The

Boy from

Tower of the Moon

The
Boy from the
Tower of the Moon

Anwar F. Accawi

BEACON PRESS
BOSTON

BEACON PRESS
25 Beacon Street
Boston, Massachusetts 02108-2892
www.beacon.org

BEACON PRESS BOOKS
are published under the auspices of
the Unitarian Universalist Association of Congregations.

05 04 03 02 01 00 99   8 7 6 5 4 3 2 1

This book is printed on recycled acid-free paper that contains at least
20 percent postconsumer waste and meets the uncoated paper
ANSI/NISO specifications for permanence as revised in 1992.

Text design by Anne Chalmers
Composition by Wilsted & Taylor Publishing Services

Library of Congress Cataloging-in-Publication Data

Accawi, Anwar F.
The boy from the Tower of the Moon / Anwar F. Accawi.
p.   cm.
ISBN 978-0-8070-7012-3
1. Accawi, Anwar F. — Childhood and youth.
2. Lebanon — Biography.
I. Title.
CT1919.L48A253   1999
956.9204'3'092 — dc21
[b]   98-48921

For Moneer

The
little
b r o w n
boy sat at
the feet of the
eyeless old man
who lived under the
carob tree by the vil-
lage spring and said,
"Grandfather, who are we,
and what is this world that we
live in?" And the old man said,
"This world's a hatchery for young
gods, my son, for that is what we are.
It is boot camp. This is where we get
our basic training before we ascend
the heavens and take our place among
the stars." And the little brown boy said,
"Thank you for reminding me, Grandfather.
I used to know that, but I have let myself forget."

The

Boy from the

Tower of the Moon

1

Anwar

My name is Anwar. I am the son of Fuad, the son of Hassan, the son of Abdullah, the son of Suleiman, the son of Andrawos the Sac Rouge. I am a descendant of the French Knights Templars, who fought the Moslems for the Cup of Christ and for the Holy Land. I was raised in the rugged mountains of South Lebanon over half a century ago. I am a pyramid builder.

I have been building a pyramid since I became aware that I was here, in this world, on this planet. That was in 1947, when I was five. It seemed the right thing to do.

The pyramid that I have been building is like nothing known to man. And although I have been working on it for fifty years, it is far from finished. But incomplete as it is now, it already stands taller than the Smoky Mountains and more massive than the Hindu Kush. However, when it is finally finished, its diamond tip will pierce heaven itself and shine among its brightest stars, my final destination.

I have been building my pyramid with my own two hands, but with the help of two hardworking slaves, Fate and her half brother, Happenstance. They quarry the boulders, large and small, and they deliver them to me. I cut them and polish them to perfection, one block at a time. Then I lay them down, stone next to stone, tier upon tier. Each stone stands for an event, each tier a year.

My pyramid is so big, and building it has taken me so long because it represents something very, very large. It stands for the story of the life of my mind — a story that began many years ago in a village called Magdaluna, that is to say, the Tower of the Moon.

2

Antar

THE TOWER OF THE MOON, my first home, stood like a watchtower upon a hill overlooking the Abulyabis River in the west and the mountains of Joun in the east. It was a very small village, the home of about a hundred people, and as far as the inhabitants of the village were concerned, there was nothing beyond the river in the west or the mountains in the east. If there was anything out there, it was too far to matter. The village had everything it could possibly need: a midwife, a farrier, a carpenter, a teacher, a shoemaker, a weaver, a vineyard keeper, and a barber who pulled our bad teeth, set our broken bones, healed us with his leeches, and bled us with his straight razor to cure our diseases.

The villagers lived off the terraced land that they had carved out of the steep hillsides. Some of them had cows, some had goats or sheep or chickens, but all of them, like my family, tended their long, narrow fields and tilled the land. And the land was kind. It yielded wheat and corn and apricots and quinces and pomegranates in abundance. There were also plenty of almonds, plums, carob, fava beans, grapes, and figs, both black and white. We ate the fruit of the earth either fresh or preserved. And we ate well. There were no hungry children in Magdaluna.

In those days the village had to be self-sufficient to survive. There was no other alternative. We did not know of any. But as close as Magdaluna came to being a self-contained microcosm, it still needed some things that it could not produce. Salt, for one thing, had to be brought up from Sidon on the coast on donkeys or mules, or the backs of lean, wide-nostriled men who were browned to a crisp by the sun. The village also needed kerosene for its tin lamps, and, on special occasions, such as All Saints Day, the village had to have fish. Abu Fareed, the owner of the only *dikkan*, saw to that.

From beyond the river he brought back, in two wooden boxes strapped to the back of his gray donkey, plenty of needle-nosed Sultan Ibrahim and *Boory* fish that he traded for sheepskins, olive oil, carob molasses, and almonds.

In the summer Abu Fareed came by every other Saturday. On those days the whole village smelled of frying fish. It was a good smell—the smell of home.

Also in the summer, a caravan of outsiders slowly threaded its way through the village. They seemed always to emerge from the mist that lay like piles of white wool on the blue mountains in the east and disappear in the foggy haze beyond the river in the west. The first to show up early in the summer were the Gypsies. They would pitch their black and brown goat-hair tents on the threshing floor, and for two weeks, they entertained the village with their music and their magic. The old, toothless, wise-eyed women read our palms and sold us sweet dreams and visions of a golden future, and the old men told us stories about heroes of old and made gold caps for our teeth. The brown Gypsy boys and girls foraged for food by begging or gleaning the fields after they were harvested.

It was a lot of fun when the Gypsies came to Magdaluna, but it was an uneasy fun because our mothers told us horror stories about them. They warned us to be careful because Gypsies were known to steal little kids to raise as their own and teach them how to beg or pick pockets or to sell them as slaves in far-away places from which the children could never find their way back home. So when the Gypsy train came to my village, I kept one fascinated eye on them and one watchful eye on Mary, my baby sister.

After the Gypsies struck their tents and left, a man from the land of *Ajam* (Persia) showed up with a huge box strapped securely to his back. We, the village kids, called it the show box. The show box had three dark, round holes in its front and three wooden legs to stand on. For two eggs, or a loaf of bread, or a pocketful of almonds, the bearded foreign man would let me and the other kids look through the holes at colorful pictures of handsome princes on horseback, delicate princesses in opulent harems, and scimitar-wielding villains in black flowing abas. While I peered through the hole, with my hands on either side of my face to block out the light, the *Ajami* chanted his tales to us. I did not understand a word he was saying, but I knew exactly what the stories were about.

The man from the land of Ajam did not stay as long as the

Gypsies did. In two or three days he moved on and, like the Gypsies, vanished in the fog that sat upon the Abulyabis River all summer long.

As soon as he was gone, the little club-foot, whom we called the Turk, showed up with his huge Russian bear. The bear was brown and had long black claws and a big metal ring in its snout. I can remember to this day how my face hurt and my eyes teared every time the Turk pulled the chain attached to the ring in order to make the bear obey him.

The show always started with the Turk playing his *daff* (tambourine). He played and sang until a large crowd gathered around him and his bear. Then he shook a long stick above the bear's head and told it to do tricks. He told it to walk on its hind legs like an old man, and the bear stood up, growled, and walked around just like an old man. The man then pulled the chain and commanded the bear to knead dough the way an old woman does, and the bear obeyed immediately. It sat down on its haunches and began to imitate an old woman kneading dough with her fists. The bear also danced and stood on its head. The last thing it did was to clap its paws and bare its long yellow teeth as if it were smiling. At this point, some of the villagers would start to walk away because they knew that the show was over and the Turk would be passing his turban around. I did not like that about my people. They wanted to enjoy the show without giving the man or his hardworking bear anything. So I gave him every piaster that I had made running errands for my father and my mother or that I had managed to wriggle out of Teta Im Fuad, my grandmother.

I loved seeing that bear every summer, and I hated to see it go, but my pleasure was tainted with the pain that I felt in my gut when I saw the bear suffer, and the hate that filled my heart for the club-foot Turk, who was cruel to his animal. I was happy to see that obscene man leave.

As soon as the Turk and his bear were gone, the tinner and his boy would show up, and all the women in the village brought their brass pots to him to have them tinned. I loved watching the ritual.

First the tinner's boy put ashes and sand into the pot, then stepped into it and began to twist his bottom this way and that. With his blackened feet, he put a shine on the inside of the pot. Then he emptied it, wiped it clean with a rag, and handed it to his father, who had been heating a tin rod in a pan over a hot fire. As soon as the tin had melted, the tinner poured it into the pot and smeared it all over the inside with a dirty cotton wad in his hand. Next he plunged the pot in a trough full of cold water. The pot hissed and sizzled until there was no heat left in it any-more. Then the tinner pulled the pot out of the water. It came out shining like a silver sun. By Allah, that was magic, alchemy at its very best. And I couldn't get enough of it. I remember squatting by the tinner and his son for hours on end, watching them transform dull-looking old pots into shiny new ones.

Once, in the summer of 1949, the tinner let me pump his bel-lows while he melted the tin. I was delighted because he let me do it, but my mama found out, and she told me never to do that again. When I asked her why, she said that it was *beneath* us to do that kind of work. I did not know what she meant by that. All

I knew was that it was fun, and I wished my father had been a tinner, too, so that I could blow his bellows and make magic with him all day long.

The last one in this parade of strangers to go through Magdaluna was the giant Moroccan medicine man. He always came in the month of *Elul* (September), just before the first autumn shower fell. He rode a huge black horse that had red tassels dangling from its saddle and blue beads (for protection from the evil eye) sewn to its reins and harness leather.

As soon as the Moroccan showed up, the whole village flocked around him to buy from him ointments for their psoriasis and boils. He also sold tree bark and herbs for colic and stomach ulcers. Some of the women, who were despised by their husbands and mothers-in-law because they could not bear children, especially male children, begged the shaman for mandrake roots to help them get pregnant. The old folk also bought from him yellowish bottles full of camphor that they rubbed on their knees, elbows, and other joints to ease the aches and pains of arthritis and old age.

When the Moroccan medicine man and his huge horse were gone, summer was officially over. After him came the first fall rain that washed away the dust of the long, hot summer. Then school would start again.

That was the way it was for as far back as anyone could remember, until the summer of 1947, the year before I started first grade in *Ustaz* (Master) Butros's one-room schoolhouse in the front yard of the Presbyterian church behind our house.

That summer, an old man wearing a red embroidered vest, black, baggy pants, and a red *tarboush* (fez) with a long black tassel, showed up, in the village square by Im Yussef's olive press, with a raccoon tied to the end of a leather thong. Nobody in the village had ever seen this man or his raccoon before.

The stranger stood in the middle of the square, and then he whipped a double-reed pipe out of his back pocket and began to play an old song called *Aladal'ona*. He was loud and he was good, and in no time at all everyone in the village came to see this new thing. Some of the villagers who were working in their fields came with baskets full of cucumbers and tomatoes hanging from the crooks of their arms.

When a large crowd had gathered around the old man, he clapped his hands above his head and sang the battle scene from the story of Antar, the beloved Bedouin hero who fought many battles and won countless victories against powerful enemy tribes single-handedly. When the song was over, everybody whooped and whistled and cheered. Then, the old man lifted his right hand and waved at the crowd. The raccoon, whose name was Antar, too, followed suit immediately. He stood up on his hind legs and waved his little black paws at us just as his master had done. The crowd roared with laughter. The old man made a circle in the air with his index finger and the raccoon did a somersault. The old man scratched his belly and the raccoon scratched his belly too. There was more wild laughter and *oohs* and *ahs* from the crowd. The man twirled around like a dervish and the raccoon rolled over, once, twice, three times. The man clapped his hands and the raccoon dropped to the ground like a rag. He lay there, flat on his back, arms stretched out, motionless. He would not move a muscle.

The old man slowly looked around at the people standing in a tight circle around him and said, "All right, folks, if you want to see Antar rise from the dead, you've got to give him something. Come on, generous people. Give Antar something if you want him to live again." Many five- and ten-piaster pieces were thrown at Antar, but he would not budge. He stayed dead until the old man snapped his fingers and said, "All right, Antar Bin Shaddad, hero of old, you can get up now."

Antar opened his eyes, raised his head a little, and surveyed the crowd. Then he stood up straight, chattering like a monkey. The crowd went wild. They clapped and cheered and whistled again, louder than before. I too jumped up and down and clapped my hands when Antar stood up. My heart swelled with joy at his resurrection. The widow Farha took a fat cucumber out of her basket and handed it to the raccoon. He grabbed it with both hands and started to eat it. He held the cucumber with both hands just like a little kid would. As he ate, small bits and pieces of cucumber fell out of his mouth on his chest. He brushed them off with his little hand.

Many remarks came from the crowd.

Someone said, "What a clever animal! I swear, by Allah, he's got more sense than Abu Jameel's twins."

Another shouted, "I have never seen anything like this in my whole life, have you?" and "By the Holy Virgin, isn't this raccoon something? Why, he is almost human, like us."

I was standing next to Abu Sameer, the lute player, and I heard him say to the old man, "Your Antar is as fat as a groundhog. You must feed him well. Is it for sale?" The old man said, "Yes, sir, he is. He sure is. I am getting too old to keep him, and my son wants me to give it up, retire, and take it easy. He's for sale."

"What will you take for it?" asked Abu Sameer.

"Twenty-five *papers* (liras) and a basket of dried figs. Not a piaster less."

"No figs," said Abu Sameer. "Forget the figs. Twenty-five liras is all you're going to get for your animal. Take it or leave it."

"No figs? No figs, you say?"

"That's right. That's what I said. No figs. That's the deal. Take it or leave it. What do you say?"

"Well, all right then. Damn the figs. You've got yourself a deal, *Ya Sayyed* (Mister)."

Abu Sameer took his money bag out, loosened the string, and carefully counted out twenty-five liras, wetting his thumb with his tongue every now and then to make sure that no bills were stuck together. When he was finished, he handed the wad of wrinkled money to the old man. The old man took the money, counted it again himself, and stuck it in his vest pocket. Then he handed the leash over to Abu Sameer. The two men, facing each other, put their hands over their hearts, bowed a little, and shook hands. The deal was done. Antar had a new master now. He belonged to Abu Sameer.

I was so happy I could not stand it. Abu Sameer lived only two houses away from ours, and the idea that he was going to keep the raccoon and I would get to see him and play with him every day thrilled me beyond measure. It was more than anything that I could have ever hoped for. It was better than Christmas.

The show was over, and the crowd began to slowly disperse, except for a few kids who clustered behind Abu Sameer and his raccoon. They followed them all the way up the hill to Abu Sameer's house.

At the gate Abu Sameer turned around and waved us off. He told us to scat. It was time for us to go home. Then he slammed the heavy iron gate shut behind him and walked up the steps to his house. Antar followed, chattering at his heels. Then they were gone.

I ran home to tell my mother about the raccoon. I described to her in detail what he looked like and what he did. I told her about Antar's little bright eyes and the black circles around them. I also told her about his ringed tail and his little black fingers and how he held the cucumber with them when he ate. She was amazed. Every time I told her about something Antar did, she would say, "How do you like that?" and, "Isn't that something?" I also told her that I was very happy Abu Sameer had bought Antar from the old man. She was happy too, and she told me that I could take cucumbers and corn to feed him, with Abu Sameer's permission, of course. Then Mother gave me my *assrounieh* (snack) which was fig preserves and almond slivers rolled up in *marquq* (a large wheat tortilla).

After I had my snack, I went back to the village square to play. There were some other kids there: Hani and his cousin Sami; Habeeb and his cousin Kameel, the goatherd's son; and Na-

seem, the carpenter's nephew. We played with tops and marbles
the rest of the afternoon, and we talked about the old man and
his raccoon. Hani, who loved to clown around all the time and
do impressions of everybody in the village, especially Master
Butros, the teacher, and Abu Ameer, the snitch, started to ape
the old man and Antar. Then Naseem handed Hani a short
stick, which he pretended was a cucumber, and Hani started to
eat it the way Antar did. We laughed and laughed until our
sides hurt.

It was starting to get dark, and I was getting hungry. It was
time to go home.

I took the gravel footpath between our house and the Presbyterian cemetery. The footpath went right by our kitchen window and, as I walked by it, I smelled the delicious aroma of meat
frying. Suddenly I was ravenous. It felt so good to be coming
home to such a smell and the promise of good eating. It had
been a great day. First there was the raccoon show, then marbles
and tops games, and now supper that smelled out of this world.

I ran into the kitchen. Mother was standing at the stove, humming, and meat was frying in the pan.

I said, "Um. That smells great, Mama. It smells so good. Will
it be much longer? Is it done yet? Can I have some?"

Mother turned around, smiled, and said, "Almost. But first,
you wash your hands, you hear?"

I ran to the deck above the cistern where we kept a washbasin
in the summer. I wet my hands, wiped them on the seat of my
pants, and ran back into the kitchen. Mama was taking a plate
out of the cupboard. She walked over to the stove and scooped

a pile of fried meat from the pan, put it on the plate, and set it down on the table, right under my nose.

She said, "Here you are. *Sahtain, Einy* (Eat it in good health, light of my eyes).

I stuck my fork in a fat chunk and brought it to my nose. The aroma was irresistible; I filled my lungs with it. Then I popped the piece of meat into my mouth. It was juicy and tender. Easy to chew. Easy to swallow.

I was forking another bite when Mama said, "You know what they say about raccoon meat, don't you? They say it is good for growing boys like you. It strengthens the heart and purifies the liver."

"Oh, yeah? I didn't know that. But why are you telling this, Mama? Why?"

"Because that's what you are eating, son. Our neighbor, Abu Sameer, was kind enough to send us some of the meat from the raccoon he butchered this afternoon. You know, the one you told me about. It was very neighborly of him to do that, don't you think?"

When I heard my mother say that, I felt as if I had been kicked in the stomach by a mule. I tried to stand up straight, but I couldn't. The pain in my guts would not let me. I clutched my belly with both hands and started to run. I did not know where I was going, but I had to run. I couldn't stand still. I ran around and around in the kitchen screaming, "Oh, God, no. No, no, no. He didn't. Oh, Jesus, you didn't. How could you, Mama, how could you? Dear God, no. He killed Antar and you cooked him. He cut his throat and you fried him. I can't believe you would do such a thing. How could you do that? How could you?"

I ran into the old kitchen cabinet that stood in the corner and slammed the door shut behind me. In the dark, inside the cabinet, I banged my head against the wall and chanted, "I do not want to eat raccoon meat. I will not eat Antar. Please do not make me eat him, please." I chanted my dirge over and over again. Outside, my mother was saying something to me. I knew she was talking to me because I heard her call my name, but it was only meaningless chatter. It made no sense. I could not understand a word she was saying, and I kept up my chant.

Then she yanked the door of the cabinet open and grabbed me by the shoulders. I did not want her to touch me, but she was strong, and she dragged me out, kicking and screaming, and hugged me tight and held me there against her. I was heaving and sniffling and she was wiping my face with her apron and kissing me on the head and patting my cheek. Then she wet a rag with cold water and wiped my face with it. It felt cool and refreshing against my skin. Slowly I began to calm down, but I could not stop shivering. My face and my hands felt hot, as if they were on fire.

Mother gave me a drink of cold water and carried me to the east room. She lay me down on the hard couch and covered me with a heavy comforter, but I still felt cold and shaky. She sat next to me on the couch and held my hand and stroked my face until I quieted down a little. Suddenly I was very tired and sleepy. She sang to me, and I started to drift off. But just before I went out, I opened my eyes, looked up at her face in the darkening room, and said, "He had a name." She said, "I know, *Habeebi* (beloved). I know. Now you go to sleep, my boy. Close your eyes and go to sleep." I did.

But when I woke up the next morning, nothing was the same as before. Sometime during the night everything was turned upside-down, and as sleep gave way to consciousness it began to dawn on me that my world, my home, was not a safe place anymore. There were people around me who were not what they seemed. They were cruel beyond anything I could possibly have imagined. That thought scared me, but what really terrified me was that not only were they heartless, they were insane. They had to be to do what they did. There was no other explanation. My God, how could anybody do what that man did to Antar and not be a lunatic? How could my mother do what she did and not be mad? Suddenly I was in terror because I realized that I was among adults who were capable of doing anything—horrible things—and not seeing anything wrong with it. But the scariest thing about it was that they had the power; they were in control, and I was totally at their mercy. I was a helpless kid, not even five yet, and there were crazy *cannibals* around me.

These thoughts did not only terrorize me, but they also made me feel dirty. Something inside me, something perfect and clean, like a red ruby, had been smashed to pieces. I did not know that I'd had it until it was gone. That morning I realized that a bridge had been burned behind me. My Eden was a thing of the past. I was exiled from Paradise forever. I could almost see the angel guarding its gate with a flaming sword.

The day after Antar was butchered, I knew I could no longer be a kid.

Because Antar came to The Tower of the Moon and died in it that summer, I placed for him in my monument a huge, white stone. I laid it in the first tier, which stood for 1947. However, Antar's stone was not the largest or the most important in that year. Many more strange and wonderful things happened and many more smooth stones were laid down to make 1947 the foundation of the pyramid that is my life.

3

The Radio

TODAY, at fifty-four, and two continents away from The Tower of the Moon, I go back in time. I find myself again standing in 1947, the first tier of my step pyramid, looking at the stones that I laid there and cemented together with my many joys and sorrows. I like what I see. The work is good. Every precious stone is in its place and time, like the notes of a symphony. If one stone were to be removed, the whole structure would collapse, just as Beethoven's Ninth or Mozart's Requiem would if one note were taken out.

Here by my foot is the stone that stands for Antar, who came to my village only to die an ignominious death and be consumed. And over there, standing taller than I, is the stone that represents the return of my father, who came back home from his roamings after the Big War, like Ulysses after the Trojan War. This stone is diamond to me. Right by its side sits a white stone brighter than Carrara marble. It stands for my father's radio, the one he brought back in the fall of 1947. I love those two stones, and I let my eyes rest on their clean lines. My mind dwells on their grace and their terribleness. And I remember.

I remember everything that happened after my father's return.

But I did not remember him very well from the years before he left. The truth was that I did not remember him at all. He had been away most of my life. My mother told me a lot about him when we sat around the *kanoon* (stove) on cold winter evenings, but I did not really know him. My father was a stranger to me. He had no place in my life.

Then one day this man, wearing a drab uniform that had the feel and texture of a cat's tongue, showed up at Grandma's house, where my mother and I were living at the time. He was carrying a duffel bag that looked heavy. My grandma and my mother were so happy to see him that they shrieked and rushed at him and grabbed him and held him tightly as if they were trying to keep him from flying away. Sometimes they took turns hugging him and kissing him, and sometimes they did it together. They cried and their noses ran and they sniffled and wiped their wet faces on the hems of their cotton dresses. I stood quietly beside them and watched.

When things began to quiet down a little, the man extricated himself from the wet tangle of women's arms and looked at me. He beamed like the sun on a June morning. My father, as it turned out, had missed me a lot and he was happy to see me. He held me in his arms and kissed me on the forehead and the cheeks again and again. He was amazed at how big I was and how much I had grown. Then he asked me if I knew who he was. He wanted to know if I remembered him. Of course I told him I did. I think he believed me. Then he told me he had something for me and asked me if I would like to have it. I nodded and said, "Yes." He reached into his bag and took out a bar of chocolate as big as a brick and handed it to me. I snatched it out of his hand and laughed. He laughed, too. And then we laughed together.

I was starting to like this man, and, I guess, I would have continued to like him had he not claimed my place in my mother's bed in the west room that very evening. This man, I was soon to find out, was not only my father, but he was also the husband of my mother.

Within a day or two I started to get used to the idea that my father was there to stay. It seemed natural for him to be with my mother like that, and I accepted it. That was the way it was with all the other kids in the village. They had mothers and fathers, too, who were also the husbands of those mothers.

So I did not mind it too much when my papa unpacked his bag, put his stuff here and there around the house, and made himself at home. I was amazed at how much stuff he had. I could not believe how many things he had crammed into that bag of his. He pulled out uniforms, shoes, belts, socks, leather gloves, shiny brass insignias, a big gun, and a brown, weird-looking box. I didn't think it was much of a box because it was all scuffed up and you couldn't put anything in it. It didn't even have a lid. But my papa seemed to think that it was very important. He handled it very carefully when he took it out of his bag and placed it in the closet by the French window in the east room.

Because I had never seen anything like it before, I did not

know what it was, or why my father handled it with so much care. I asked him about it, and he told me that the box was actually a *radio*. I did not know what that was. He explained to me that it had some special wires and tubes inside it and that those wires and tubes could pick up sounds right out of the air and play them. To show me how it worked, he turned the knob on the front of it and a red menacing eye, which was high up in its forehead, began to glow. Then it flickered on and off. My father had to tap the box gently on its side a few times to get the light to stay on. It did. Then he fiddled some more with the knob and out of the brown box came this sweet sound—this music—the like of which I had never heard.

It was as if someone had thrown open a window in heaven and through it floated down to me, like summer rain, the most beautiful sound that ever fell on human ear. That was no *tablah* or double-reed-shepherd-pipe music. It was not tambourine music either. It was the kind of music that I imagined the angels of Allah played for Him to cheer Him up and make Him forget His troubles. I could have listened to it forever. But my father abruptly turned it off and the red light slowly faded away. I begged him to let it play some more, but he wouldn't turn it back on. He said that he had to save the batteries, those little yellow things he called Rayovacs in the back of the radio. He told me that batteries were expensive and very hard to come by. They had to be saved for more important things like the *news*. I did not know what he was talking about, but I suspected that news had to be something much more wonderful than music. Why else would my father want to save his batteries?

I did not have to wait very long. I found out what the news was the very next day after my father's return. Christ, was it a letdown. I just about never got over it.

But the radio and the news turned out to be a big thing to the village people, especially the grown-ups and the old folk. That became evident shortly after my father's return to the Tower of the Moon.

Magdaluna was everything a village was expected to be after a major war. It was divided and obscenely poor, and there was scabies everywhere. Scratching was as common as breathing. The politics of war had torn the village apart the way hyenas tear a carcass. There were those, like Abu Wajeeh, the gunsmith, who thought that Hitler was the best thing that had ever happened to the world since Attila the Hun, and there were others, like Khalil Yussef, the only deacon at the Presbyterian church, who believed that Winston Churchill was the Messiah Himself come back incognito. Political views and allegiances were so strong that the men of the village named their sons after Axis and Ally leaders. Magdaluna had a Hitler and a Mussolini, as if the world did not have enough of those. There was also a Bernard, named after Field Marshall Montgomery, the British officer.

Poverty, as it always does, made even worthless things very precious and cause for disagreements and feuds. The inhabitants of Magdaluna were no exception. Take, for example, the Daghers and the Mussas. These two families fought like a pack of howler monkeys, but over what?—a small piece of land that was literally eaten up with brambles and bushes. The Mussas were convinced that this piece of earth was *musha'* (communal property), and the Daghers claimed that it had been in their family for generations, since before the Turkish hordes had invaded Lebanon.

By the end of the war, the intensity of the hatred and resentment that those two families harbored for each other, though no blood had been shed, had reached a feverish pitch. And because Magdaluna was such a small community and everybody was related to everybody else by blood or marriage, the dispute made life a living hell for many. Some marriages were strained to the breaking point, especially when the husband and the wife fell on different sides of the issue. The children were also dragged into the fray, and it wasn't uncommon for brothers and sisters to belong to opposing camps.

When my father came back to Magdaluna with his meager possessions and a lot of war stories, the village was a sick community in more ways than one. Young as I was, I could see the conflict. But in keeping with ancient custom, the whole village put aside all its enmities for the time being and came to my grandmother's house to welcome the return of Fuad, her native son, who had been off to war those many years.

It was late October. On the evening of the second day after my father's return, the villagers started to show up at our gate. Some, like Shukri, the retired Turkish army drill sergeant, and Saleem Hanna, the consumptive widower, who never did a day's work in his whole life (according to Grandma), came by themselves. Others came in twos or threes, and many, like the younger folk, came in noisy groups large and small.

Grandma's house, I heard my father laughingly tell my mother in the kitchen, where she was making Turkish coffee for our guests, reminded him of Noah's ark, especially the cargo.

Our guests gathered in the east room, where Grandma usually received respectable company. They came to express their joy and their relief at my father's safe return and to listen to his war stories. They sat around the room on three long, rickety sofas made from the coarse lumber of shipping crates by Abu Bassam, Magdaluna's only carpenter. The sofas, which were lined up against three of the walls (the eastern wall had a huge French window in it) had thin cushions stuffed with corn husks, which made them hard. Grandma's choice of corn-husk stuffing was not due to the lack of other more humane materials because she had, up in her attic, where I used to hide and play, many bags full of feathers plucked over the years from enough chickens to feed a retreating Turkish division. I think Grandma used corn husks on purpose. She was a one-eyed, no-nonsense Presbyterian with a frightful work ethic, and she did not want any of her visitors, including the red-nosed preacher she was sweet on, to get too comfortable and stay long.

"There are more important things to do with one's time than to sit around and gab," she would slap her thigh and say. "Time does not wait for those who sit around on their behinds and let their lives seep away like water in the sand. What will they say to their Master when He asks them about the talents he'd given them? You tell me. What?"

So Grandma, for religious reasons, stuffed the cushions of her sofas with corn husks, and it worked. No visitor who was not paralyzed from the waist down could have sat on those sofas longer than fifteen minutes without going numb. Half an hour would have stiffened the toughest ass, but those were hard times, and many a bottom had been toughened by hard living. So, we all had a long evening to look forward to.

Above the sofas, in neat parallel rows upon the wall, there were faded black and white portraits of dead Accawis on my grandfather's side and dead Suleimans on my grandmother's side. And in the smelly, dancing lights of the two tin kerosene lamps in the corners, the rows of frozen people staring down from their frames at the rows of stiffened people sitting beneath them on the hard sofas created an eerie sight, juxtaposing those who were already dead with those who were already dying. Thick smoke rose in wisps and swirls from the cheap tobacco of the hand-rolled cigarettes like the smoke of hideous offerings made in dark and slippery temples unto pagan gods.

Because of the radio my father brought back with him to Magdaluna, that scene was to be repeated many more times before the summer finally came around and brought with it a respite from the crowds, the smoke, the body odors, and the fear of disease, which relentlessly haunted my fastidious mother.

I remember how terrified my mama used to be because many of our visitors were sick. She constantly worried about me, her firstborn son, catching some loathsome disease from the village people who, by the end of the war, had become a museum of rare and exotic diseases. My mother used to mark the cups and saucers in which she served tea or coffee to anyone whom she suspected of having TB, scabies or gum disease, and later she would boil those cups and saucers in hot water until, as my father used to say jokingly, they became soft and tender.

In keeping with ancient tradition, many of the distinguished village men (who had a lot of sheep or goats) stood up in turn to honor my father with speeches, and some of the more eloquent old-timers got to do that twice or three times that evening. It was in the middle of the third round of Welcome-home-to-the-people-who-love-you-son and We-are-proud-of-you-and-what-you-have-done speeches that would have gone on and on until the cock crowed twice that my father decided he'd had enough. So, he stood up and announced to the crowd that he had brought back with him . . . a radio.

When the people heard that pronouncement, they froze instantly, as if they had just looked into Medusa's eyes and turned to stone. Hands gripping coffee cups stopped in midair between shiny, threadbare pants knees and lips puckered in anticipation of hot sweet things. All coughing, sneezing, sniffling, blinking, and throat clearing was suspended as if the announcement had paralyzed the very nervous systems of those emaciated and unwashed bodies. They became as quiet as chickens when a hungry hawk circles the air above their heads. Even the acrid clouds of cigarette smoke that filled the air seemed to hang motionless in the silence. No one dared to break the spell of the hush, not even the Presbyterian deacon. Only my father could because he was the Man—the proud owner and operator of the first radio ever to come to The Tower of the Moon.

The Man did finally break the silence, just as it was becoming intolerable. He left his seat and walked across the room, over to the closet in the wall by the French window. Very slowly, he turned the handle on the closet door, and then, for dramatic effect, he quickly flung the two doors of the closet open. There was a loud sound of sudden breath intake from the crowd when the brown box between the two faded yellow curtains was unveiled for everybody to see, and many hands rose to cover many mouths in a gesture of reverence, surprise, and disbelief. Two old women, Im Michel and Im Fareed, made the sign of the cross. Necks craned, eyes squinted, spectacles were nervously readjusted, and bottoms half rose from the hard seats. My father turned the radio's one knob on, and the red eye glowed like a charcoal ember in the dark. There was another faint ah from the crowd, and many more hands rose to cover many more mouths.

The silence was shattered by the sound of static that crackled like bacon frying in an overheated pan, and in the midst of those frying sounds was heard a distorted voice that faded in and out as if it were coming from far away over the raging waves of an angry sea. But it was a strong voice, and it sounded very important "BBC . . . the news . . . London . . . Her Majesty the Queen and Prince Philip . . . preparations . . . royal . . ."

The news did not interest me, and I went looking for a place to lie down. Mother was too busy playing hostess, so I went to Grandma, climbed into her lap, and went to sleep.

The evening of the following day was a replay of the night before, only this time more people came because the word had gone out to all the neighboring villages that Fuad Hassan Accawi, the son of Mariam Suleiman Mussa, had come back from the war and brought with him a radio.

At about five minutes to six, my father opened the closet door and turned the radio on. Again, the red eye glowed and again, like the night before, there were oohs and ahs and the sound of shuffling feet. There was also a lot of pocket watch checking and resetting done to the resounding bangs of Big Ben. I believe Magdaluna was the only village for miles around that had synchronized timepieces long before the other villages woke up to the wonders of our changing times.

Of course, in those days accurate timekeeping was not a priority with the villagers. Time did not mean that much to anybody because no one was in a hurry to get anywhere or to do anything. Hell, the whole village looked unfinished. There were half-finished and abandoned projects everywhere you looked: houses, chicken coops, walls, you name it.

Pocket watches, which every respectable man in the village had to have, were not valued because they kept good time; some of them did not even work. They were nothing but toys—interesting gadgets and status symbols. Who needed them to keep track of time when the one thing that everybody seemed to have a lot of on their hands was time? If a field was not plowed on Monday, it could be plowed on Tuesday or Wednesday. If a mule needed to be shod on Saturday, there was no point in breaking one's neck to do it. It could wait until Monday when the weather might even be nicer. *Bukra* (tomorrow) was the most popular word in the lexicon of Magdalunians. So the radio that my father brought with him to the village did not give Magdaluna a new sense of urgency, nor did it affect the slow rhythm of life in the village. But it did bring something else to Magdaluna, something the village needed much more than news of the outside world or accurate pocket watches; it brought togetherness to a people who had been divided for years by bitter hatreds and petty differences.

Night after night, the villagers came to Grandma's house to listen to my father's radio and to keep in touch with a world that was changing around them at dizzying speed. When they came, they had to sit together in Grandma's small guest room. And, as was expected of them under her roof, they had to be civil to one another and show their hostess respect. They had to eat and drink together what they were offered, and when their eyes met, they had to speak. Once they had spoken, they began to change, and Magdaluna was the better for it for a while.

Because of the radio, Ameen, the son of Yussef Mussa, met Samira, the youngest daughter of Hanna Dagher, fell in love with her, and married her. Their wedding brought their warring families close together again, and there was peace. Because of the radio Saleem Hanna's health improved, and he was no longer bedridden, waiting for that sweet chariot to swing low and carry him home. For weeks, Saleem had reason to get out of bed every evening and oil his steel gray hair and put on his Sunday clothes and his *tarboush* (fez) and inch his way, sweating and gasping, all the way up the hill from his house to Grandma's to catch the BBC evening news. About the third week, he stopped using his cane, his color got better, and his appetite came back (Grandma noted grudgingly). He even started taking long walks around the village because, he said, it felt great to be able to do that again.

In a couple of months the batteries got so weak that the radio could not be heard from across the room anymore. But the healing magic of the radio was not diminished at all. If anything, it got more powerful because the weaker the batteries became, the closer everybody huddled around the radio. By the end of the second month, the closet was no longer visible when the radio was turned on because everybody gathered tightly around it to get their daily dose of the dope.

At one point the batteries got so weak that only my father could hear what was coming over the radio, and to do that he had to stick his head into the closet. Then he would relay what he'd heard to those around him, who in turn would pass it on to the old folk who were hard of hearing.

Of course there were times when there was a complete breakdown in communications, and the old folk who sat on the outer limits of the huddled mass received some very strange messages from the closet, like the time it was announced that the British in Palestine were turning away European Jews who were seeking refuge in the promised land. By the time the news was relayed from the closet to Abu Mikhael, who was sitting by the door, resting his chin on the handle of his walking stick, it had been completely distorted. You could see the confusion in the man's eyes when Im Wadi shouted into his cupped hand, which he held shakily around his translucent ear, that the British were turning into Jews and seeking refuge in Palestine because the Europeans were chasing them in big boats.

My father had to do something about this. To remedy the situation, he had to boil the batteries. That prolonged their lives a little bit, and he did manage to get a couple of news broadcasts after that which came across loud and clear, but that was it. The batteries had had it. They were dead. So, my father had to talk Grandma into buying him some because he was broke. He had a hell of a time getting her to sell a few kilos of almonds to Abu Fareed, the storekeeper, so he could send for a set of batteries from Sidon on the coast, the nearest town around. She finally gave in and gave him the money to get his precious batteries.

About two years after my father and his radio came to Magdaluna, Khalil, the son of Raheel, returned from Argentina to see his dying mother, Sarah, and he brought with him one of those newfangled transistor radios that you could hold in the palm of your hand. After his mother died, Khalil sold his little radio to Majeed, the son of the mayor, and went back to his wife and business in Argentina. The village split immediately after that because there were two radios to listen to now. The evening crowd at Grandma's house got thinner and thinner week after week.

Then Samar, the preacher's nephew, came back from Beirut, where he was going to school, with another radio, even smaller than Khalil's, and before you knew it, those damned things were all over the village. They seemed to multiply faster than blue-lipped, barefoot, drum-beating Gypsies at a country wedding. It got so you could buy one of those things, made in Taiwan or Korea, from any shop in Sidon for ten dozen eggs or a few bushels of olives or a tin of virgin olive oil.

Eventually my father's one-knob radio went the way of the inkwell. There was no need anymore to huddle together in Grandma's east room to listen to the news, to argue about politics, to check the time and reset pocket watches, or to speculate about the economy or the weather or anything else. There was nothing left to bring all the people of Magdaluna together under Grandma's roof every evening. Now everybody could get their music and their news whenever and wherever they wanted. Even the little shepherd boys and girls had them, and while they watched their flocks of sheep and goats in the fields, they held their radios in their little brown hands or dangled them from a cord around their thin, sunburnt necks.

God, how I missed the noise and the crowds, the hustle and bustle of people coming and going, the smell of Turkish coffee mingled with cigarette smoke, the occasional pat on the cheek, the chance to hold an old-timer's cool pocket watch in my hand and watch its hands move and feel its heart ticking. Christ, how I hated the quiet evenings at Grandma's and those infernal transistor radios, those cheap, scratchy, noisemakers that took my village away from me and robbed me of so many friends.

I do not know what happened to my father's radio that sat behind the faded yellow curtains in the closet by the French window. It may have ended up on Magdaluna's garbage heap or it may have been buried under a lot of junk in Grandma's attic. Maybe my father traded it for a pack of Bafra cigarettes or a bottle of *arrack* (a strong drink made from grapes). Or he may have sold it to Abu Ameer, the village tinkerer and snitch. But it seems to me that I lost track of it about the time Uncle Fareed came down from Jordan to be at Grandma's funeral. Because he loved me, he brought me a little present—a transistor radio with a cord to hang, like an albatross, around my neck. I thanked him when he slid the cord around my neck. And then I cried. He was delighted. He thought that my tears were tears of joy. I never let him know how I felt about his present to me.

In time I began to enjoy my father's being around, and I got over the disappearance of his radio. I also got a little tougher too, and two more polished blocks were added to the pyramid of my life.

4

Dinar

JUST AFTER my father's return, Grandma Mariam, who liked me to call her Teta Im Fuad, gave me one of her chickens to keep as a pet. I named her Tawza (the tailless one) because she had lost her tail feathers to a gray fox in a close encounter a few weeks before.

Tawza was not a young chicken, which was unusual at Teta's house because Teta killed her chickens and fed them to us while they were still young and tender. Every Saturday she would go out into her little farm and chase down an ill-fated rooster, wring its neck, and stuff it with rice and almonds for Sunday's dinner. Teta's first choice was young roosters because she believed that male animals were good for nothing but to be eaten. However, when young roosters were in short supply, she relaxed her standards and went after her hens. But Tawza survived. Her life was spared for two reasons: because I liked her very much and because she regularly laid double-yolked eggs. Every morning Teta Im Fuad would fry me one of Tawza's eggs in virgin olive oil and sit across the table to watch me, with her one good eye, clean my plate.

This routine went on for some time until one day Teta told me that Tawza was getting ready to *sit*. Sitting, according to Grandma, was putting a bunch of eggs under Tawza for a few days to make more chicks. But sitting, as I was soon to find out, meant going without double-yolked eggs in the morning. I did not mind very much because there were other layers on the farm and plenty of other good things to eat: quince preserves, homemade goat cheese, black olives, and apricots.

While Tawza sat, I checked on her five or six times a day to see if any chicks had hatched. After a few days I began to despair of ever seeing her progeny, so I cut my visits down to two or three times a day.

Tawza's sitting dragged on and on for what seemed like a whole summer in Sunday school. I was just about ready to give up on ever seeing her offspring when it finally happened on a cool morning in the month of *Tammuz* (July).

I was awakened at dawn by the thump-thump-pat-thump sounds of someone making bread on the *saj*. Actually, it wasn't so much the noise that woke me up as the smell of fresh bread baking. I got out of bed and staggered, barefoot, to the shed where my mother and my Teta were baking the weekly supply of wheat tortillas. It was a crisp morning, and the dirt felt good beneath my feet. The sun hadn't come up yet, and there were no sounds coming from the village. Magdaluna was still asleep. But sound travels on cool, quiet mornings, and that was probably why I heard the faint cheep, cheep, cheep of newly hatched chicks. Curiosity instantly banished hunger. I forgot all about the hot fresh bread and ran to see the new arrivals.

But instead of a whole brood of little yellow chicks crawling everywhere, there was only one. And he was beautiful. I squatted down to get a closer look at him, and he peeked at me from under his mother's breast where he was snugly buried in her speckled feathers. He was not afraid of me. I could see that in his little bright eyes. We looked at each other for a long time before I got up the courage to reach out and touch him carefully on the head. He let me do it, and I loved him for it.

This was better than having a birthday. I had gotten many nice things on birthdays before—wind-up toys, cap guns, and a sling shot—but nothing I had ever been given made me feel the way that chick did that July morning. Because he was small and yellow, like a gold coin, I named him Dinar (a gold coin).

Right from the start, Dinar and I became inseparable. I guess he thought I was a member of his family, an overgrown brother or a cousin, and he followed me around, like a puppy, everywhere I went. Sometimes he followed me so closely that he would trip on my feet, flap his wings, and fall flat on his face. I had to be careful not to step on him, the way his mother did every now and then. As he followed me around, I would scratch for him in the dirt with my finger, as I had seen his mother do with her beak, and he would run to see what goodies I had uncovered for him to eat. I gave him water to drink and crushed wheat to eat. He learned to eat right out of my hands, and sometimes he went to sleep in them. He would squat down in my cupped hands, fluff his feathers up and close his eyes. Dinar was the only one for whom I would sit still. I did not make a move until he'd had his nap. While he slept, his little claws held tightly onto both my finger and my heart.

I got to keep Dinar for only two weeks. It couldn't have been more than that because Abu Fareed, the man who sold sardines from the two smelly boxes strapped to the back of his donkey, came by regularly every other week. Those two weeks were among the happiest times of my life. Then disaster struck.

It happened on a sizzling afternoon early in the month of *Ab* (August). The heat was so intense that, in the distance, the houses, the trees, and the mountains looked like they were dancing in the haze. The whole world looked as if it were sagging and getting ready to melt, like wax, in the oppressive heat. Even the silence was hot and wet, and it brought no comfort to either man or beast. The wind was dead. Nothing stirred. And then the muggy silence was suddenly ripped by the cackling and squawking and other fowl noises that only terrified chickens can make on a hot August afternoon.

Everybody in the house was doing the only thing there was to do on a hot summer day, sleeping. Only I, like a mother who knows the cry of her baby in a roomful of squalling babies, recognized Tawza's distress call and responded immediately. In the blink of an eye, I was off to the rescue, with Grandma's cane in my hand and murder in my heart. I was ready to kill anything that was terrorizing my Tawza.

When I got to the mulberry tree, where the racket was coming from, I found nothing. I couldn't believe it, but there was nothing, not even a tomcat slinking about or a chicken hawk circling above.

"Darn, a false alarm," I thought to myself. "Better get back inside where it is nice and cool."

Just as I turned around to go back inside, the flutter of tiny wings among the exposed roots of the mulberry tree caught the corner of my eye. I looked closely and saw Dinar thrashing about wildly. That silly little chick must have gotten his head stuck in the roots while chasing after a bug or a worm. It was so much like him to get into a jam like that. I leaned Teta's stick against the tree and reached down to free him when, to my horror, I saw that the root in which Dinar was stuck had a lifeless, glassy eye and it was looking straight at me. Then it moved.

I jumped back as if I had stepped, barefoot, on a scorpion. My heart started racing; I could hear it pounding in my ears. My temples began to throb. My throat tightened, and a very old anger, mixed with fear and hate, kicked in deep inside me and took over my hands. They grabbed Teta's cane and went to work as if they had a life of their own. Blow after expert blow landed on that loathsome, writhing thing until the tears and the sweat pouring into my eyes blinded me and I could no longer see what I was striking at. When I finally stopped to catch my breath, I could barely see through the blur that the glass eyed thing was now a wet scaly lump.

My Dinar lay beside it, motionless. I grabbed him and looked at his limp body. He looked so much smaller than he did before. I did not know what to do, so I told him that I was sorry and that I loved him very much. Then it came to me to rub his chest right under the wings to get him to breathe again. While I was trying to revive him, I wailed, "Oh, Jesus. Please, Jesus," but to no avail. He would not move. He just lay there in my hands, tiny, ruffled, and wet. For a moment I hated him because he would not respond, and I hated God because He would not hear my pleas.

Waves of despair, as cold as the north wind in January, washed over me as I stood alone under the mulberry tree with my dead Dinar in my hands. This was final, and I knew it. All the love and prayers in the world could not bring him back. He was gone, and I wanted to be dead too.

Mother woke up when she heard me crying, and she rushed to my side to help me and to comfort me. But I was feeling so miserable that her hugs and kisses brought me no comfort at all. That filthy snake not only killed my little friend that day, but it also took away from me, forever, what little healing magic had remained in my mother's kisses after Antar's death.

Later that afternoon, while I slept from sheer grief and exhaustion, Mother buried Dinar in the soft dirt in the western corner of a small patch of fava beans. She covered his grave with a heavy stone because she did not want anything to disturb him anymore. She told me what she had done when I woke up about dinnertime.

I was only five when I lost Dinar, but I knew then that when it came to the things that really mattered, I would always be alone. And I accepted that.

The boulder that stood for my Dinar and his death was as big as a shepherd's hut. It was so heavy that it took both Fate and

Happenstance to deliver it to me. They were reluctant to do it, though. But I received it and went to work on it and polished it for a long, long time. Then I placed it in the first tier of my pyramid where it belonged, next to the radio and the raccoon. It fit perfectly there.

Words

My EYES move on beyond Dinar's yellow stone and stop at a marbled black and white block, rectangular in shape, slim and quite tall. It looks rather light, but it stands with a dignity and certainty all its own. I love it more than any other stone in my unfinished pyramid. It is my most favored. I speak to my stone and tell it the deepest secrets of my soul with no reservations, tell it that I remember everything about our first encounter as a man recalls every detail of that moment when he was stunned by beauty and grace. And I swear to it, with a solemn oath, that I will honor it and give it all my devotion as long I shall live, because it gives me my life; in it *I live, I move, and I have my being.*

The name of my idol is the written word.

We met on a cold, rainy afternoon, about two months after my father's return to Magdaluna. I had come into the kitchen for some sweetened hyssop tea when I saw my father sitting at the old kitchen table with a white sheet of paper in front of him and a porcupine quill in his hand. I saw him dip the quill in a bottle that had a black fluid in it. Then he made some marks at the top of the sheet. The marks looked like chicken scratches to me. But I got curious.

I got closer to him and said, "Baba, what are you doing with that quill? Are you trying to draw something? What is it? Tell me. What?"

He said, "No, I am not drawing anything. I am writing a letter to my brother Fareed. You know, the one who lives in Jordan."

I did not know what the word *writing* was. I had never seen my mother or my grandmother do anything like what my father was doing.

I asked him, "What's that? What is writing? I don't know what writing is."

"Well," said my baba, laying his quill down on the table, "WRITING, er, let me see, writing is drawing words. You draw them with pen and ink on paper. The words we speak have shape and form, like everything else in the world."

"How did you know that?" I asked. "Did your mother teach you their shapes? Did she?"

"No, she didn't. Your grandma doesn't know how to write. I learned writing in the little school in the churchyard, the one you'll be going to next year when you are five."

"Does every word we speak have shape? Every one? There are so many of them. Nobody can remember all of them, can they? Did you have to memorize all the words? You didn't, did you?"

"Oh, no. You don't memorize the shape of every word. You just learn the shapes of the letters, and when you have learned them, you use them to draw the words."

"Letters? What are letters? What do they look like? How many of them are there? Fifty? More?"

"No, not that many. There are only twenty-eight letters in Arabic, the language we speak."

"Well, what are they? Can you teach them to me? Will you show me what they look like, will you?"

My father lifted me up and sat me on the table. He drew the Arabic alphabet, all twenty-eight letters, on a piece of paper. He drew them all, from alif, a, to yā, y. Then he showed me how to put some of them together to make words. He spelled my name, Anwar, and it looked great. It was one of the most beautiful things I'd ever seen. He also taught me how to draw the words *mama, baba,* and *Teta.* I practiced writing these words until evening came.

When I went to bed that night I had with me the sheet of paper on which I had written my first words. I went to sleep feeling strange, as if a window had been flung open before me and I was looking through it at a world I had never seen before—a wonderland that had no end.

And when I woke up the next morning, my world was suddenly full of the written word. It was everywhere. On the chest in the east room was Teta's big, heavy Bible (that she had to have, but could not read), and in the closet, on the shelf above the radio, were the books that my father had brought with him when he came back home. There were so many of them that they filled the whole shelf. I remember standing in the east room that morning and looking at those books and wondering whose names were written in them and whose stories. I longed to know, I needed to know. They were mysterious writings. And I could feel their power.

However, the most powerful writings I saw after my father taught me my first letters were on the two yellow sheets my Teta (a term of endearment that means grannie) had hidden in a tin can under a lot of junk up in her attic. She took them down to look at them one day, when the two of us were alone at home. I saw them in her hand and asked her what they were. She said they were *deeds* to her property.

"Deeds? What's that? What do they say? Is your name written in them? Are they important?"

"Yes, my name is written in both of them. These papers say that I own this house and the olive grove by the village spring. They are mine, you know."

"By Allah! These papers say you own stuff? Nobody can take it away from you? Is it yours forever?"

"Yes, it is mine. I have the papers to prove it, too. It's all mine. These papers say that. The house and the olive grove and everything else named in these deeds belongs to me."

This was too much for me to take. In Teta's little house there was a book in which the words of Allah Himself were written. In the closet there were books that held between their covers the stories, the thoughts, and the feelings of men and women who lived far away and long ago. My Teta had, in her attic, yellow papers that said she owned a house and land. What power! What magic! What is this wonderful thing, the written word? I did not fully understand, but I was in awe of it and I was in love with it.

That love has gotten wider and deeper over the last fifty years. I guess I am an idol worshiper. Only my god is not gold or fame or power, like the gods of some other men. Mine is the written word because that is where my life lives. To honor it, I have placed its symbol, that marbled black and white rock, in the pyramid that stands for the life of my mind—human and divine.

6

The Gramophone

THE WRITTEN WORD is my first and last love. I need it as
much as I need the air I breathe and the water I drink. But it is
not my only love. There are other objects of worship in my life.
Two of these are the camera and the gramophone. In my pyramid their stones stand immediately above those of the radio and
the raccoon. They are special stones because they look as if they
had been cut out of huge pearls. I am glad that Fate and
Happenstance found them and brought them to me. They are
like rests in a musical score. Without them the composition
would be incomplete. Without them my pyramid cannot be
perfected.

Fate was the one who brought the camera to me in the spring
of 1948, the second *mastaba* (tier) in my pyramid. Later, her
brother, Happenstance, would deliver the gramophone. They
did not come as themselves, of course. They hardly ever do. But
I realized who they were immediately because I knew how
those two clowns operated. I was familiar with their modus ope-
randi. So, they did not fool me at all when they showed up dis-
guised as Uncle Wadi, my father's youngest brother.

That spring, Uncle (Aammo) came up from Beirut, where he was going to school, to see his mother, Grandma Mariam, and to spend some of his Easter holiday with us. It was great to have him home again. He was a lot of fun because he always showed up with fascinating new gadgets, and he would take the time to tell me what they were, how they worked, and what they were used for. He was the one who gave me my first sheep-horn pocket knife, and he was the one who introduced me to the gramophone, the kind that you wind up with a crank.

Easter Sunday was Resurrection morning, and as good a time as any to have a religious experience, which I did.

After a sumptuous dinner of chicken stuffed with rice and almonds and a tasty yoghurt and cucumber salad, Aammo announced, in a mock-ceremonial voice, that he would be taking pictures of those who wished on the deck above the cistern. As soon as I heard it, I made a dash for the deck, followed by Mary, my little sister, whose new dress made swishing noises like the rustling of leaves every time she moved. We both limped a little that day, as we always did on holidays, because our shoes were stiff and they gave us blisters.

Because I was the firstborn male in the family, I got to go first. Aammo made a big thing out of posing me, telling me to smile and to tilt my head this way or that to catch the bright spring light.

The air crackled with excitement. My hands trembled. My breathing became shallow and rapid. My knees felt deliciously weak. I felt very much the way I did the first time I sneaked into the Catholic church, against my father's express instructions, and smelled the incense and heard the priest chanting in a strange and melodious language as he stood in the warm glow of candlelight, swinging a smoking brass bowl that dangled like a yo-yo from the end of a yellow chain. I remember shivering a little when the priest's eyes met mine, and I knew right away that he knew I was Presbyterian. The feeling that came over me was like nothing I had ever felt before. It was a mixture of excitement and fear. I loved it.

That Easter morning I had the same feeling again as I stood under the unblinking gaze of the two-eyed black box in my uncle's hands. It wasn't that I had never seen photographs before, because I had, quite a few. The walls of the east room in Grandma's house were plastered with the pictures of dead men and women who sat stiffly with their hands on their knees. It was just that I had never thought about how those pictures were made, or what they were made with. I had never seen a camera before, not until that Easter Sunday in 1948.

There I was, standing in the presence of a man who was about to snatch a moment from an ever-vanishing world and hold it forever. Like Joshua, whose story Grandma had told me time and time again, my uncle was poised and ready to freeze time and stop the sun dead in its tracks. I was so excited that I forgot to breathe.

I was only a kid at the time, yet I knew that I was partaking of something strange and wonderful, and not totally without sin.

I felt a little *sinful* about having my picture taken because my Sunday school teachers had drilled it into my head that making images of any kind, be they statues or photographs, was sinful.

They said that those things were idols like the golden calf that the Hebrews worshiped in the desert. They told me that images were evil, that they should be destroyed. (There was, however, behind the pulpit in our church, a wooden cross with a bronze Jesus crucified on it. But one day the bronze Jesus disappeared. I guess it either fell off or it was stolen. The preacher said that it was just as well because the vacant cross now symbolized the risen Messiah).

I guess what I had been taught in Sunday school was the reason for my feeling a little guilty that day as I stood in the April sun waiting for Aammo to make an image of me. But I did not give in to my guilt or fear. I stood my ground and waited until Aammo finally pressed the little silver button on the front of his black box. When he did that, I heard a faint click. I could have sworn that one of the glass eyes, the one on the bottom, blinked. It winked at me and I was bewitched. Right there and then, I fell in love with the camera. It has been a lifelong romance that has only gotten sweeter with the passing of the years. The picture that Uncle took of me that day would remain in the family for many years to come, until the onset of the Lebanese Civil War in 1975. Then, like our books, music albums, and Byzantine coin collection, that photograph would be lost in the haste and the confusion of our flight from Sidon.

Uncle Wadi came back to the Tower of the Moon late in the month of August. He and three of his friends, one man and two women, came up from college in Beirut. They rode up in a fast-moving wagon they called an autobus from Beirut to Kittermaya, a village on a hill about five miles northwest of Magdaluna. In Kittermaya my uncle and his friends hired a mule skinner who owned the mule and the two donkeys that they rode the rest of the way to Magdaluna. They arrived at Grandma's house on a Friday afternoon. I remember that very well because my mother was getting everything ready for our weekly bath on Saturday morning, while Teta was chasing her roosters to kill them and stuff them for Uncle and his guests. I suspected that those people were important because Grandma went after her biggest and fattest birds.

When Uncle and his company arrived, my father helped one of the women, the one with the short red hair, get off the mule. The other woman swung her leg around above the donkey's head and jumped off like a monkey. Her long brown hair flew behind her in the wind when she leaped. I liked her on the spot and I wished my uncle would marry her. Grandma, Mother, and everybody else in the village said that it was time for him to find a good woman and settle down before he lost the rest of his hair. I think Uncle was in no hurry to do that. I suspected he was having fun because he came back to the Tower of the Moon many times with many different women. I think my father was kind of envious too. He tried hard not to let it show, but I saw the way he looked at my uncle's women friends when he thought nobody was watching. I guess he thought I was too small to notice and he didn't have to be very careful around me. I saw that look in his eyes, but I never ratted about him to my mother. I knew that my baba loved my mama.

In keeping with the village custom, Grandma offered to feed the mule skinner and his animals, but he turned her down. He said he had to get back to Kittermaya before it got dark and the hyenas came out. So Uncle paid him and he left in a hurry. But I could hear the jingle of the bells on his beasts for a long time after he left.

While it was still light and dinner was cooking, Uncle Wadi invited his friends to take a walk around the village. He wanted to show his company the old Catholic church with the stained glass windows and the natural spring where the whole village got its drinking water. He asked me if I wanted to come along. I was happy to join them on their walk. Maria, the long-haired woman, held my hand as we walked around. I guess she did not want me to fall down and hurt myself when we hit the rough spots in the road. I didn't need her help, really, because I knew every inch of my village and I was as agile as a billy goat. (My mother said that I even smelled like one sometimes.) But I enjoyed holding hands with Maria; she smelled like jasmine after a rain.

I did not like the other woman very much, although she had pinched my cheek and kissed me hard on the mouth when she first arrived and Uncle introduced me to her. I did not like her even though she told my uncle that his nephew was so cute. She was squeaky, and her long red fingernails pricked like the *shaytan's* (devil's) trident.

After seeing the village spring and getting a drink of fresh cool water, we headed back to the house. Walking had made us ravenous.

We ate outside on the deck above the cistern. Mama and Grandma had cooked chicken and grape leaves stuffed with rice and almonds. There was also hummos (chickpea dip) and a garden salad with my favorite homemade dressing—lemon juice, garlic, and olive oil. Dinner was great and everybody was having a good time. My baba even let me have some of his *arrack* mixed with a little water, and I felt wonderful. But the best part of the evening was yet to come.

After dinner, Turkish coffee, and smokes, Uncle went looking for his bag. Then he came back with a strange-looking box. I could see right away that it wasn't a radio, like my father's. But I couldn't even guess what it was, so I asked Uncle. He said it was a gramophone. I asked him what that was, and he told me to wait and see.

Mother cleared a place on the table and Uncle set his box down. Then he opened the lid and gently leaned it back. After that he took what looked like a matchbox out of his pocket and opened it. Carefully, he took out a needle and stuck it in the knob at the end of an arm inside the box. Then he let the arm rest on a little cradle. That done, he produced out of his bag a shiny black plate. It wasn't much of a plate because it was perfectly flat, like the palm of your hand. He laid the plate down in the box and, using a crank on the side of his box, he started to wind it up.

I looked at the faces around the table, but nobody seemed to be paying any attention to what Uncle was doing. They were talking and drinking and laughing. I was the only one interested and puzzled by the box and the ritual my uncle was performing right before my eyes. When he was done cranking, he lifted the arm with the needle on its tip and slowly brought it down on the black plate. As soon as he did that, the plate began to spin. I was wondering what kind of wind-up toy that box was and what it was going to do when the needle touched the plate. At first I heard some scratchy noises, and then there was music, wonderful music, like that which came out of my father's radio, music that came from the same *sama'* (heaven).

My father said, "It's been a while since I've heard this one. It sure brings back memories."

Uncle said, "I knew you'd like it. It's one of my favorite tangos, too, you know."

"Oh, mine too," squealed the short-haired woman. "I just love it, don't you?"

Well, I did, and I wanted it never to stop. I wanted it to play on and on forever, but it didn't. The plate began to spin more and more slowly, and Uncle had to crank his box up again. Then he stood up and reached out for Maria's hand. She laughed and got up and hugged him tight. She hugged my uncle and my ears got hot. I had never seen anything like that before. Men and women did not do things like that in Magdaluna. When they danced at weddings or baptisms they held hands in a long line and stomped the ground with their feet, but they did not embrace—never, at least not where everybody could see them. Again I looked around the table and nobody seemed to think there was anything wrong. I began to relax a little bit.

I sat back in my chair and let myself enjoy the show. Maria and Uncle were a sight to see. They danced and danced as if they were one. Every move they made was right. Every step they took was perfect. I felt so light watching them, I could have floated on air.

When Uncle put another plate on, the music was even sweeter. My father asked my mother for a dance, but she said no. Baba insisted, but she wouldn't give in. She said she liked the music but she wasn't crazy about that kind of dancing. The Lebanese *Dabki* (foot stomp) was what she liked. The tango she did not much care for. So my baba asked the other woman for a dance. Her boyfriend wasn't feeling up to it, and she accepted. That evening I got to watch my baba do something I never thought he could do. He danced like a whirling dervish. And the redhead was like a rag doll in his arms. She looked like she had no bones in her body. My baba twirled her, spun her, dragged her, and flung her around until I got dizzy, but he always caught her just before she hit the floor. I could not believe my eyes. My father was better at this tango thing than my uncle could ever hope to be. The moves that he and that redhead made were absolutely amazing, and I wondered what other things my father could do that I didn't know anything about.

Uncle played a few more disques (that was what they called those flat black plates), but nobody danced. We just sat around the table, nibbled on things and listened to the music and talked. Then mama told me to go to bed. I did not want to, but she made me.

Uncle and his friends left on Sunday. He said he had classes on Monday morning and he couldn't afford to miss them. Abu Asaad, the farrier's cousin, had a couple of donkeys, and he took

Uncle and his friends back to Kittermaya, where they would catch a ride on the autobus back to Beirut. I hated to see them go, especially Maria. I hoped to see her again many more times, but I never did. She never came back to the Tower of the Moon. My mother said that Maria gave up on Uncle Wadi because he would not promise to marry her.

When Uncle Wadi went back to college, he did not take his gramophone with him. He left it and a stack of his disques with us. He said he wanted to get a newer model that ran on Rayovac batteries, like my father's radio. Boy, was I glad he'd left it behind. And then I wasn't.

Shortly after Uncle went back to Beirut, the young ones in the village heard about the gramophone. They would come to our house in the evenings and listen to it. My father taught a couple of them—Noha, the miller's daughter, and Bahij, the stone mason's son—how to do the tango. They learned fast and then they taught others. This was the kind of music they wanted to listen to. This was the kind of music they wanted to dance to. *Franji* (European) music was what their hearts desired, not the Lebanese *Dabki*. That was old-fashioned, something to leave behind and forget.

Before Uncle Wadi's gramophone came to Magdaluna, the whole village used to gather at the threshing floor on balmy summer nights. The old folk came to watch the *Dabki* and clap their hands, and the young ones came to dance and have a good time. Everybody stayed until the moon sank into the sea. My mother used to take me with her to those dances, and I got to watch her and her young, beautiful friends dance like silver ghosts in the moonlight. The music of the double-reed pipe was haunting, and the *tablah* beat to the twinkle of distant stars. God, how I loved the music, the dancing, and the smell of the dust mingled with the smell of young, warm bodies. Sometimes, when the moon was full, I even got to see a thing or two when a young man, thinking that no one was looking, planted a hurried kiss on a girl's smooth cheek.

I watched everybody and saw everything as I sat on a block of stone with Magdaluna's cannonball at my feet. The old-timers, like Abu George and Abu Asaad, said that the shell was lobbed by a British frigate from the Mediterranean at some Ottoman soldiers holed up in Chehim, a village farther up in the hills. But the ball fell short of its target. Fortunately, it was a dud, and the young men dug out the gunpowder inside it and stuck a piece of bent oak wood in the hole. After that they used it as a test in their rites of passage. When a young man was able to lift it above his head with one hand, he was a grown-up and he was accepted in the company of adult men. Every now and then, between dances, one of the young men would walk over to the cannonball and raise it above his head, then drop it with a mighty thud, leaving a deep dent in the ground. Sometimes the young man, after dropping the ball, would ruffle up my hair and say, "Come on, Nour. Let's see you do that now. Grab that cannonball and lift it above your head."

And I would get hold of it and strain with all my might to budge it, but I could not, even when I used both hands. All I could do was just roll it around a little. Then everybody would laugh good-naturedly and go back to do the *Dabki* and beat the threshing floor with their feet until it shuddered. I felt it tremble through my feet, and I longed to be a big man among men with a black handlebar mustache the size of a ram's horns under my nose. I yearned for the day when I would be able to lift that cannonball without even breathing hard and then go on to dance the *Dabki* with the other men and women until dawn.

I never got to. All that came to an end long before I reached the age of nine. It stopped forever after that cursed gramophone of my uncle's came to the Tower of the Moon. The *tablah* fell silent, and the wailing of the double-reed pipe no longer echoed from the surrounding hills on starlit summer nights. Then the grass, like a flood, reclaimed the threshing floor. It grew thick and defiant and green, and the cannonball disappeared. One day it vanished, just like that, as if someone or something had yanked it out of the village because it was no longer needed or wanted there. Its days were over, finished, for new things, far better things, had come to the Tower of the Moon.

I did not think I could stand it. Even today, when I think about that loss, a hard pain, like fingers of steel, grips my heart and squeezes until the tears pop out of my head.

In memory of that death I have, with my own two hands, cut a black stone for my uncle's gramophone and set it in the pyramid of my joy and my pain. But it is good, all of it, good; even the bad is good. Because of it I am what I am today.

Mama

THAT SAME SUMMER, just before the twins, Mona and Moneer, were born, I got my first Spanking. As mischievous Fate and twisted Happenstance would have it, I had to have my beating on what had to be the most beautiful day in August.

It was warm, bright, and clear. The sky was a pale blue, and the clouds that drifted across it looked like the big piles of white feathers that Grandma stuffed in her cushions and pillows. I couldn't stand being inside on a day like that. I wanted to go out and play with the boy who lived in the big stone house with the red tile roof at the end of the gravel road by the Catholic church.

I asked my mama to let me go. She said it was all right. But first she had to put some nice clothes on me. I knew what that meant, and I braced myself for what was coming.

Mother walked over to the blue closet that stood by the window in the west room. She opened it and carefully studied the row of clothes she had neatly hung up for me. Humming to herself, she picked the outfit she was going to put me in. She took out a green shirt that had sailboats all over it and a pair of white shorts that were ironed to a knife-edge. She inspected them by the light coming in through the window. (My mother was the kind of woman who did not believe that cleanliness was next to godliness. In her book, cleanliness *was* godliness.) The outfit she had picked passed. She then began the dressing ritual, which involved a lot of pulling, tucking, smoothing, and tugging. It seemed to take forever. When it was finally over, she brushed my hair vigorously to a sheen. I felt as if I were being scalped. Finally, Mama wet her thumbs with her tongue and smoothed my eyebrows with a firm sweep. Then she stepped back, squinted her eyes, and took a long critical look. Satisfied with her handiwork, she smiled and said, "Now you are ready to go play with your friend. You may ride his tricycle if he lets you, but remember to ask him politely, and whatever you do, don't mess up your clothes, you hear?"

I promised my mother that I would be polite and careful. Then I took off before she had a chance to give me another one of her thorough inspections. I was on my way to play with my friend who lived in the big house with the red tile roof.

His name was Issam or Azzam or something like that. I don't know why I have trouble remembering his name, but I have never forgotten how he looked. He was very thin, and his skin was so pale that the blue veins in his temples stuck out like exposed roots in a riverbank after a hard rain. The corners of his mouth were always wet, his eyes teared constantly, and he sniffled all the time. Whenever I saw him he was wearing a sweater, even in the summer, and his mother, who was a big woman, was always chasing him around with a green bowl full of white mush. She constantly begged him to eat. (It was rice pudding I suppose, because "it's the only thing his mother knows how to cook," my mother would say scornfully.)

Issam lived behind a wall with a huge iron gate in the middle of it. The wall was so high that I couldn't see anything even when I craned my neck and stood on my tiptoes. The gate had, high up in the middle of it, a yellow knocker that I could not reach. So I picked up a rock and banged on the gate a few times. There was no answer. I banged again and again until I heard footsteps. I knew they were Issam's because they were as light as a bird's. Slowly the iron gate squealed open, barely enough for me to slither through.

Behind the gate stood Issam, doubled over, with his hands resting on his knees. He was wheezing and his chest was heaving. Opening the gate to let me in had left him completely exhausted. When he recovered a little, he straightened up, wiped his eyes with the handkerchief that he carried around in his sweater pocket, and started back up the narrow tiled path toward the house. I followed him, and he took me around the back into the garden.

It was like stepping into a fairyland. There were flowers everywhere: yellow roses, pink carnations, red snapdragons, and jasmine that smelled so sweet it made my head feel light. In the middle of all this color was a fishpond teeming with fat red fish, lazily swimming around and around in silent circles. Suddenly a tremendous sense of well-being came over me. I felt that everything was going to be just fine that afternoon.

I was right. It turned out to be my lucky day because Issam, who usually clung to his tricycle like an octopus every time I came over to play, was feeling worse than usual. Sensing that he was in no shape to give me any trouble, I helped myself to his tricycle. He did not try to fight me for it. He didn't even tell me to stop. All he could do that afternoon was stand and watch as I rode his tricycle all over the garden, around the fishpond, and under the almond trees. I rode until I got tired of it.

About an hour later, Issam's mother showed up with her green bowl to give him his snack. I had done enough riding for one day, and I was ready to go home for *my* afternoon snack, too.

On the way home, I decided to take the footpath that went around Issam's house in the back because I wanted to see what the old bachelor who lived in the little yellow house was up to.

He was somewhat of a mystery man in our neighborhood because he was hardly ever seen out. When Mother and her friends used to get together to drink coffee, they always spoke in whispers when they were talking about him. I was curious and I wanted to sneak a look at him on the way back home. I made the detour although my mother had warned me many times not to go near that man or his house. She made me promise to stay away. I asked her why. She said he had TB, a horrible disease that gets into your lungs and eats them up.

I was terrified by what my mother told me, and I made up my mind never, ever to catch TB. That was the one thing I wasn't going to do.

But that warm, sunny afternoon, curiosity overcame fear, and I broke my promise to my mother and to myself. I walked back home by the old bachelor's house, only to wish afterward that I hadn't. No, I did not catch TB and die coughing up blood. I wasn't that lucky. It was much, much worse.

When I got to the corner, just before the yellow house, I started walking on my tiptoes because I did not want to wake up the little deadly germs that were sleeping in the dust. When I rounded the corner, I had a wonderful vision. I saw a pile of fine sand on the sidewalk, right in front of the old man's house. It was a huge pile, and it sparkled like gold in the afternoon sun. Then to my utter delight, the sandpile called me over, saying, "Come and play with me. Come, let's have some fun."

I responded immediately and jumped into it with both feet. It was warm and I lay in it and rolled around the way I had seen chickens and horses do in the dirt. The sand felt good and I buried myself in it up to my neck. Then I built castles and roads and bridges, which later I destroyed gleefully with a kick of the foot or a sweep of the hand. After that I started to throw handfuls of it in the air and watched it fall back down like rain, making little rainbows in the sun as it fell. Suddenly there was sand everywhere—in my hair, in my undershorts, in my mouth and in my eyes. It hurt, and I had to go home. Pain has always driven me there, only that time the real pain was waiting for me at the house.

When I got to the door I kicked it until my mother opened it. As soon as she saw me, she put her hand to her mouth and slammed the door shut, as if she had seen the devil himself standing at her door butt-naked. There was a worrisome pause. A moment later, she opened the door again and peered at me. I guess she was hoping to find that she was wrong about what she had seen. But she wasn't. It was her son standing at her door, and *it* was filthy.

Mama stood there for a while and glared at me with eyes as big as saucers. Then she began to sob. I did not know how to deal with the situation because I'd never made a grown woman cry before. But there she was, this big woman, angry and weeping before me. I couldn't see why. There was nothing wrong with me. I was not bleeding. My head was not bashed in, and I wasn't missing any eyes or teeth. Suddenly she stopped crying. She wiped her eyes on the backs of her hands, straightened up, and her back stiffened. Then she grabbed me by the arm and, like a spider, jerked me into the house. She took me to the kitchen, sat down on a chair, and laid me, bottom up, across her knees. Then with the flat of her hand she went to work on my behind. She hit me so hard I thought I was going to pass out. She was healthy and she was strong because she had spent most of her life on the deck beating the dirt out of her rugs with a cane. She made every blow count.

When the beating was finally over, she gave me a bath in the metal tub that we kept on the deck in the summer. It was one of the longest baths I'd ever had. She used a new loofa on me. It was rough, and she rubbed me hard with it as if she were trying to remove my skin. I think that she got soap in my eyes on purpose, too. When my eyes started to burn, I got up and ran into the yard. She chased me all over it trying to catch me, but she couldn't. I was all soaped up and as slippery as a sardine, but she finally cornered me between the outhouse and the chicken coop. And she finished what she was doing. All I managed to do, by running away, was to prolong the bath because I had fallen once or twice while I was dodging her and got dirty all over again.

When she was satisfied that I was clean, she took me out of the tub and towel-dried me with vengeance. I was as red as a beet by the time she was done with me. Then she put a long, clean T-shirt on me, and carried me back to the kitchen. She sat me down at the kitchen table and gave me a glass of milk and two *biscottis* (cookies), which I took to be an antidote for TB.

Later, after she had cooled down a little, she sat me in her lap and hugged me and kissed me on the head and ran her fingers through my hair. She sang to me my favorite song, the one about Ibrahim, the little shepherd boy who had a magic bamboo flute that made the wishes of little boys and girls come true.

I was surprised at how good I felt, considering that I had just survived a vigorous attempt on my life.

She smelled warm, and I softly drifted off to sleep.

Mama's love was tough. And I learned to take it with my chin up. I respected her because she was a survivor, and she was also a fighter, especially when it came to preserving her dignity and protecting her family. She was, as my father put it, a regular lioness.

During The Big War, my father met her in Qamishly while he was traveling with the British army around Syria's inhospitable deserts. Qamishly was a remote village on the Turkish-Syrian border. It was a tiny haven for a few minorities who spoke among themselves half a dozen dead or dying languages. There were Armenians, Assyrians, and Kurds to mention a few.

My mother's mother was a hard, domineering, closed-mouthed woman who would not say much about her origin or how her husband, my grandfather, was killed, but it was rumored that she was a Russian immigrant who fled to Syria sometime during the Bolshevik Revolution of 1917.

When my father's unit rolled into Qamishly, Nazira, my mama, was twenty-five and quickly getting to that age when she would be considered *unmarriageble*, a spinster. Also, she'd had enough of her mother, who had constantly kept her under her thumb. When Fuad, my baba, showed up in the town square looking sharp in his British uniform, Nazira was ready to do something about her situation. Fuad had two things going for him: he dazzled her with his Lebanese charm, and he was her ticket out of that Syrian hell.

Within days from the time they had met, they were married and on their way to Damascus, the fairest city in all of Syria. Nazira never did go back to see her mother in Qamishly. Her mother died around the time I was born in 1943. I never got to meet my maternal grandmother, something that I do not regard as much of a loss, considering what I'd been told about her. That is why there is no stone in my pyramid for her.

After a short stay in Damascus, Fuad brought his foreign wife to his mother's house in Magdaluna. Within a week he had to leave his bride and go back to Syria to rejoin his unit. Mama was left to face her new life alone, among strangers, in an alien village. She also had Mariam, my tough grandmother, to contend with. But having had to deal with her own mother, Mama was ready to take on Grandma. From the very beginning, Nazira made it clear to Mariam that she was not going to take any shit from her. Grandma Mariam made a couple of feeble attempts to put Nazira in her place, but she got nowhere fast. After that, they got along fine. Even as a little kid I could sense the respect that my grandmother had for my mother when she spoke to her. And in no time at all, Grandma Mariam learned to call my mother *Habeebti* (beloved) and *Nour Einy* (light of my eyes). My mama called her mother-in-law Mother, and that was that.

However, my admiration for my mother is not based solely on her being a survivor or being protective of her own. I admired her because she was knowledgeable, wise, and well-educated. The fact that she was illiterate did not at all diminish her stature in my eyes. If anything at all, it made me appreciate her more, because she knew so much in spite of the fact that she could not read or write. My experience has confirmed to me over the years that a formal education is not necessarily a true education. My mother was a doctor of philosophy without a college degree. Her eyes were open, her heart was vigilant, and she was willing to learn. That made her a great teacher, my teacher.

Today, as I stand by my pyramid in the setting sun of 1997, I recall one of those unforgettable learning moments that my mother and I had early in the fall of 1948, when I noticed that her belly was huge. It seemed as though her stomach had ballooned overnight. So I asked her about it.

She said, "My tummy is big because there is a baby growing in there."

"What's his name? Does he have a name?"

"No, he doesn't have a name. Your baba and I haven't picked one for him yet."

"How long has he been in your tummy? Has he been in there long? Does it hurt a lot?"

"Almost nine months. Since last Christmas. And no, it doesn't hurt at all. Actually it feels rather nice."

"Well, how did he get in there, into your belly, I mean?"

"Your baba put him there. Babas do that, you know. Mamas can't have babies without them."

I drew a blank. I could not see what babas had to do with mamas having babies, or how they managed to do it. All I could do was ask how my baba did it and when, for Pete's sake, when? I was always around my father, but I'd never seen him do anything that remotely resembled inserting a baby into my mother. Doing that would have taken some time, and my father would have had to use something from the kitchen or the toolbox in the attic. And where on earth did he get a baby to put inside my mother in the first place? I had to have some answers.

"You know, when you and Grandma go to sleep in the east room? Well, your baba and I lie down together on the same mattress on the floor in the west room."

"All right, what's that got to do with it? Why are you telling me this? Does anything important happen then, while I am sleeping?"

"Yes. Little things come out of your baba *down there* [pointing to my *down there*] and they get into me, and that's how babies get started. These little things look like tadpoles.

Yes, little black tadpoles. That's what they look like. You know, tadpoles like those you see in the pond by the village spring? One of them is enough to start a baby."

"One tiny little tadpole is all it takes to make a baby? That's it?"

"No, not exactly. I haven't told you about the egg. You see, mamas have lots of eggs inside them."

At that point, I looked up at my mother's face to see the twinkle in her eyes, the laughter hidden deep behind them. She had been pulling my leg all along and I fell for it. What an idiot I was. She made up this unbelievable story about invisible tadpoles that got into her and made babies grow inside her, and now she's telling me about eggs? What a story! How could she lay eggs like Tawza, my pet chicken?

"You shouldn't do that. You are making fun of me," I said on the verge of tears. "You lied to me. You lied."

"No, I did not. Every word I've told is the truth. Come here. Give me a hug. I am your mama, and I love you. I wouldn't lie to you. You've got to believe me. If you do, you'll grow up to be a very smart boy. You see, I can't tell you everything I know now because you are too little and you are not ready to understand everything. But what I've told you is the truth. Believe me."

Well, there I had it, all the information my head could hold, but still I had no idea how it worked. There were still many things that did not make any sense.

After giving it a lot of thought while playing in the carob tree, I decided that the egg was a tiny baby, already finished. But it remained asleep until the tadpole came in and woke it up the way water wakes a fava bean and makes it sprout. That's how it had to happen. Nothing else made sense.

And I was right! It was just as I had thought. The twins, Mona and Moneer, were born late that August. Im Fadel, Magdaluna's only midwife, pulled them out of my mother just after sundown. Mona came out first, and she was as tiny as a skinned squirrel and as blue as an indigo cube. Im Fadel handed her to Grandma Mariam and some old toothless crones who had gathered in the east room to help. They worked on Mona until she coughed and cried. Then she turned pink, and the old women yodeled and clapped their hands. Moneer was twice the size of his twin sister and he refused to come out. He fought the midwife every inch of the way—I watched the fight through the kitchen window—but Im Fadel was a woman to be reckoned with. She was a tough old widow who had the arms of a lumberjack and in the end the baby lost. As soon as he was out, Im Bassam dashed out of the west room to tell my baba that the second baby was a boy. He wept for joy because in those days boys were highly prized, even above gold and silver, in the Tower of the Moon. The neighbors joined my father in his rejoicing: they fired their rifles into the air—boom, boom, boom—and the night echoed their reports over and over again as if it were joining in the celebration. Then many bottles of *arrack* were uncorked and passed around, and the whole place smelled of anise. Someone's hand in the dark offered me a drink. I took a big swig. After that everything became a blur. I remember nothing.

I woke up the next morning. Somebody had laid me on a

couch in the east room. My head felt heavy. I had to hold it up with both hands to keep it from rolling off my shoulders. Then I remembered the night before and the twins. Barefoot, I rushed into the west room to see my little brother and sister. Mama was sitting up in bed having a cup of hot milk. She looked tired but peaceful. The twins were lying side by side on two big pillows over a sheepskin. They were wrapped up in white sheets. Their eyes were closed, but every now and then their nostrils flared, and the white sheets rose and fell.

Mama said, "They are beautiful, aren't they, Nour?" I nodded my head without taking my eyes off them—my new brother and sister. I said, "Can I touch them? Is it all right if I put my hand on them?"

Mama said that it was OK. But she told me to be gentle. I put my hand on my baby brother's head. It was soft on top. I could feel his heartbeat under the palm of my hand. That got me worried, and I said to my mama, "He's not finished, Mama. The baby is not finished yet. His head is soft. He came out too soon."

Mama laughed and said, "No, he didn't, *Habeebi*. He's finished all right, down to his little fingernails. That's just the soft spot. All babies have them when they are first born. Didn't you know that? You had one too, you know, when you were a little baby."

"I did? My head was squishy like this when I was born?"

"Yes, it was. But you're fine now, aren't you?"

"I guess so. Why are babies born with soft heads like my brother's? Why?"

"So they can grow. If the head bones are soft, then the head has room to grow, you understand?"

"Okay, I guess. Can I smell him now, Mama? Can I, please?"

Mama giggled and said, "Of course you can. Go ahead. There is nothing like the smell of a newborn baby, nothing."

I leaned over and sniffed my baby brother's head. It smelled sweet and warm and unforgettable. Forty-eight years later (and a world away from Magdaluna, our old home), I would still remember how my baby brother's soft spot smelled when I leaned over him in the intensive care unit of a Birmingham, Alabama, hospital and kissed him on the head. It was very warm—feverishly hot—because his body was desperately fighting the toxin that a fire ant stinger had shot into it on the previous Easter Sunday. My brother's brain was dead. It had died two days before, but his body, with the help of a respirator, was still fighting for dear life, and I remembered how his soft head smelled when I was five and he was only one day old.

For a long time after he died, I did not think I could bear the pain. But I did, because I am the son of Nazira Suleiman Mussa Accawi, my mother, my teacher. From her, I had learned to survive and to be strong. She prepared me well.

Because my mother taught me many wonderful things about honor and courage and integrity, I have set her stone in the corner of my pyramid. No other place would have done her justice.

8

Teta

My mother was my first teacher, but she was not the only great teacher in my life. There were many others, but among them all only Teta Mariam, my grandmother, was in a class of her own; she was my mentor. She knew people, and she was aware of the inner workings of her society and the souls of men. From her I learned that human beings are fickle. She said that they were changeable; they would love you one day and hate you the next if their interests conflicted with yours, especially in matters of money. She also told me to be the best that I could be at whatever I chose to do.

I remember her one day sitting on the deck above the cistern and weaving a *tabaq* (place mat) from yellow, blue, and red straw. It was a fall day before school started and there was nothing for me to do. I squatted opposite her to watch what she was doing. It was like watching a Gypsy magician. She turned straw into wonderful things, and she did it so well.

I said to her, "Teta, what you're making is so beautiful. Who taught you to make things like that? Did you learn it from your mother?"

She said, "Yes, my mother showed me how to work with

straw, but I can do it better than she ever could. That's right, better than she ever could."

"How come? How can you be better than your teacher? Is that possible?"

She sighed, looked up from her work, and fixed me with her one good eye. Then she said, "I got better at this than my mother because I wanted to. That's how. You see, Nour Einy, if you want to be good at what you do, you can, and if you want to be the best, you can, too. If you are good you become a hill, but if you are excellent you become a mountain."

"What's the big deal? What's so great about being a mountain, Teta?"

"If you are a mountain, then you do not need anybody's approval. You are there, big and immovable, and people will have to deal with you. You don't have to deal with them. You know, like Abu George, the farrier."

"What about him? What about Abu George? Is he a mountain? Why? Why is he a mountain, Teta?"

"He is a mountain because nobody anywhere for miles around can shoe horses and mules the way he can. Nobody. That's why they come to him from all over to ask him to shoe their animals. They beg him to do it because they know he's the best. And they await his pleasure. You know Abu George, he does what he wants to do when he wants to, not when someone else wants him to. That's being a mountain, *Habeebi*. You understand? Do you?"

"I think I do. Are you the best, too, Teta? Are you the very best at anything? What is it? Tell me."

"Well, my olive grove yields more olives and olive oil than

anybody else's in the whole village. It is not as big as some of the other olive groves, like Abu Majid's and the widow Farha's. But mine puts out the most oil and the biggest, fattest olives. Everybody here knows that. Didn't you?"

"No. I had no idea. I know that the big jars in the kitchen are full of oil, but I didn't know that your olive grove was the best. How do you do it, Teta, how?"

"I keep the dirt around my trees broken up and soft, and I use the chicken droppings from the chicken coop. I know how deep and how far to put the droppings from my trees. You see, if you don't know what you're doing you can burn up your trees or starve them to death. You've got to know what you're doing, son. You've got to know what you're doing."

So when I went to school later that fall, I made up my mind to be the best I could be. I wanted to be excellent, and I was. It wasn't that hard, really. All it took was for me to do my best every day. When I did my grammar homework it was neat. When I did my additions and subtractions they were neat, too. I checked and double-checked all my work, and Master Butros, my teacher, told my grandma, when he came to eat stuffed chicken with us, that my work was excellent.

But being excellent was not all that Grandma taught me. There were many other wonderful and inexplicable things she passed on to me. For example, she knew where Allah lived.

Grandma was a Presbyterian, and as far back as I can remember, she always started her day by reciting the Twenty-third Psalm. Every morning, rain or shine, she would throw the French window in the east room wide open and look up at the hills and say, "The Lord is my shepherd, I shall not want." I used to stand by her side, hold her hand, and repeat after her, word for word, what she was saying. Then the sun would burst from behind the Monastery of Christ the Savior in the mountains of Joun, and the day would begin. Sometimes, before she went to the kitchen to make breakfast, she would stand there and look at the hills for some time, and then she would say, "The Lord God lives in those hills. He loves mountains, you know." I had no idea what she was talking about. How she knew where God lived was a mystery to me. But that was what she told me time and time again.

Grandma taught me many more things that helped shape the life of my mind. From her I learned that God was accessible. He was not far away where He could not be reached. She prayed to Him all the time, but she did not pray the way the preacher at our church prayed or the way other people prayed at mealtimes or funerals. They prayed as if the God they knew wasn't listening or was deaf or far away someplace, and they had to raise their voices to get Him to hear what they were saying. They begged and pleaded with Him as if He was reluctant to do any good thing, and they had to talk Him into doing stuff for them. Grandma did not do any of those things. She just talked to God as if He was standing right there in the room with her. She told Him things the way she would tell a friend. One day I heard her even forgive Him. I did not know that you could forgive God, but Teta did. She forgave Him for letting her eye be taken out a few years back.

Grandma had been bitter because she had lost her eye when

she was still young and attractive. She was picking green olives for pickling, one late summer day, when a leaf swooped down like an arrowhead from the top of a tree and stuck her in the eye. The cut was tiny, barely visible, nothing to be concerned about. But it got infected and her eye had to be taken out.

It took Teta many years to sort that one out, but she finally did when I was a little older than five. I was there to hear it and see it when it happened. She put it behind her that day and never mentioned it again. Grandma had finally managed to set herself free.

Teta was also very generous when it came to giving to the church. When the olives ripened in September and were taken to Im Yussef's olive press, she made sure that at least one tenth of her thick green virgin oil went to the church. She also gave the church almonds by the *ephah* (basket), wheat by the bushel, and pomegranates and fava beans and everything that the good earth put out. She never missed church on Sunday morning or on Wednesday night. And she fed the preacher well. At her dinner table he ate many of her fat, tasty chickens stuffed with rice and almonds. When my mother or my father said something about her giving away too much, she would wave her hand in front of her face and say, "You don't have it until you give it away." It would be many years before I began to understand what she meant by that.

But it wasn't many years before her faith was tested the way Job's was, and worse. That was in the spring of 1948, my first year in school. That was also the year in which she got *that disease*. Mountain folk in Lebanon called cancer *that disease* because they were afraid to say the word. They believed that by saying the word they would bring the sickness upon themselves. I don't know what Grandma did to bring that horror onto herself so swiftly and unexpectedly. Early in the winter of 1948 she began to complain to my mother about the pains she had in her legs. Sometimes, she said, her legs would go numb under her. My mama told her that she was probably overdoing herself and reminded her to take it easy because she wasn't a spring chicken anymore. But the first chance Mama had, she sent word to Uncle Wadi in Beirut. Uncle made arrangements for his mother to come down to the American University Hospital. Grandma was gone for a week.

When she came back she had with her a bag of painkillers to help her die painlessly. The cancer in her spine was inoperable.

The painkillers stopped working after a while and Grandma was in a lot of pain. She was a tough woman, but there were times when the pain made her scream the way a horse does when it stumbles and breaks a leg. Within weeks she lost the use of her legs and had to lie on a rubber sheet on a mattress on the floor in the west room. I watched her suffer and I wondered why her God-friend, the one who lived in the mountains east of our house, wasn't helping her. Sometimes I just could not bear to see her that way or listen to her scream or moan. That was when I ran away to be alone and to think in the peace and quiet of my secret hideout.

A few months before, I saw a hare in the field behind the school. I chased it around until it disappeared behind a mulberry bush at the foot of a mound the size of a pile of wheat at

threshing time. I followed it there and found a small hole in the
rock, completely hidden from view by the bush. I went down on
my knees and stuck my head into the hole to see what was in
there, and the world turned upside-down. I felt that my head
was inside something as deep and wide as the night sky in winter. I got a little dizzy, the way I did on cool summer nights when
I lay flat on my back on the deck and looked at the stars until the
world turned over and I was looking down at the stars below me.
I had to stop before I fell into endless space. I pulled my head
out, took a deep breath, and waited for the world to stop
spinning.

As soon as my head cleared a little, I stuck it back into the
cave to take another look. When I did that, a very strange feeling
came over me. I felt old or, rather, ancient, as old as the cave
itself, more ancient than the cedars of Lebanon. My heart
raced. I could hear it pounding in my ears. I did not know what
to make of this weird feeling. So, I just sat there, at the mouth of
the cave and waited for that odd sensation to go away.

When I felt steady again, many thoughts started leaping
about in my head, the way grasshoppers do when a hunting dog
suddenly runs into a grassy field. But my first and foremost con-
cern was whether anybody in the village knew about the cave.
My mind told me that no one did because I had never heard
anybody say anything about it before. Not even old-timers like
Abu Wajeeh, the gunsmith, or Abu George, the farrier, who
were given to yarn-spinning and who knew all there was to know
about the Tower of the Moon, had ever mentioned it before.
None of the kids that I played with knew it was there either. I

would have known about it if they had. I supposed that I was the only one in the whole village who knew that cave was there. I was overjoyed. The fact that I had discovered a cave that no one knew about not only thrilled me, but it also gave me a sense of power that made my heart swell inside my chest.

Then paranoia set in. It was all over me like red chiggers on a hot August afternoon. I felt the way a prospector does when he pulls out a two-pound gold nugget from a river bed only to discover that he is standing among a bunch of cutthroats. What to do? What to do? Then resolution came to me like God's lightning, swift and nonnegotiable. No one was to know, not even Albert, my cousin and best friend. And that was that.

The thrill of discovering the cave and the vow of secrecy just about wore me out. I felt tired and decided to go home. Exploring the cave would have to wait until the next day. And there was thinking to be done and plans to be made.

The following day was a Sunday. I had neither the time nor the appetite to eat the usual Sunday breakfast of *marquq* bread, fried eggs, *labneh* (homemade cream cheese), *zaytoon* (olives), and hyssop tea. I hurriedly made a *labneh aroose* (sandwich), grabbed a candle and a box of matches, and stuck them in my back pocket. I was off to explore my cave. I was there in the time it took to eat the sandwich.

The mouth of the cave was small, but I was small too, and I had no trouble crawling in. As soon as I was inside, I struck a match and lit the candle. Then I took a look around.

The inside of the cave was huge. It was about three *qamats* deep, (a qamat is the height of a man), two qamats high and two qamats wide. The ceiling and the back wall were covered with a wet, shiny stuff that looked and tasted like salt, and when the candle light fell on it just right, it made little rainbows like those I had seen in a kaleidoscope which Emile, my second cousin had brought back with him from Africa for his grandmother's funeral. The floor was a soft reddish-brown. It looked as if someone had mashed a lot of crayons with a roller like the one we used to pack limestone with on our roof to keep it from leaking. Here and there on the floor lay dead, dry leaves and twigs, blown in by the *Gharbia* (westerly wind).

Fortunately, there were no bats living in my cave, but it was the home of a quiet, brown spider and a colony of big black ants. I did not mind sharing my cave with them. In fact, having them around taught me a lot about them and about myself.

The first thing I did was to get the cave ready to move into. I set the candle on a rock ledge and, with a small branch I had cut from the mulberry tree, I swept the leaves and twigs into the corner. I knew that someday, when the weather turned cold, they would come in handy. With the candle in place and the floor clean, my cave was ready for my move.

The next thing I had to do was move all my stuff to my new hideout. The cave was just the place to hide my things away from the other kids because they were not above taking them if they wanted them badly enough. I moved my treasure—a cardboard box full of empty shotgun shells that my father had used hunting quail, and a handful of copper coins that were no longer in use. I also brought over my slingshot, which my cousin Albert had made for me from an oak branch and a red inner tube, and the storybook that my uncle had given me for my birthday.

It took me three days to move all my stuff to the cave. I did not want to do it all at once for fear of attracting suspicion.

Right from the start my cave became the center of my world. Inside were hidden all the things I held precious, and it was the place I could go when I needed to be alone. Sometimes I went there just to get away from my little sister, who expected me to play with her and take care of her while my mother did her housework or drank coffee with the women from our neighborhood who came to talk about other women in the neighborhood. Sometimes I just had to get away to think. It seemed that there was always something happening to keep me busy. Either my mother wanted me to go to the *dikkan* to get her a bag of salt, or my father wanted me to get him a pack of cigarettes or a fifth of *arrack*, and sometimes my grandmother asked me to fetch her a drink of water or her flyswatter or her bedpan. There was always something to keep me from thinking a thought through.

In my cave I could pick up a thread and follow it without any interruptions, all the way to Damascus if I had to. That day, when I ran to my cave to be alone, the thread I picked up was grandma's sickness, her inevitable death, and how her God fit into all that.

The thing I could not understand was why would God, who was Grandma's friend, let her suffer the way she did. I wanted to know why He was not lifting a hand to help her. She loved Him and sang psalms to Him and gave lots of stuff to His church and fed His ministers, but He didn't seem to remember any of that. He wasn't there for her, as if she didn't matter or He didn't care.

I thought and thought about all the reasons why He was doing nothing for her. Finally, I came up with only two possible answers: either He couldn't or He wouldn't. I could understand the first reason. Her God could not help her because He was incapable of it. Cancer was too much for Him to do anything about, and I could understand that. But then He would not be the Almighty that I'd heard Grandma and the preacher say He was. If He isn't, He is just one more sorry, powerless god like the idols the Phoenicians worshiped in the surrounding hills.

The other explanation for His doing nothing for my dying grandmother was that He didn't want to. If He could but refused to, it meant He didn't care. If that was the case, Grandma had been a dupe. She'd let herself be fooled into believing that He was her friend.

The thought made me furious. I got restless. I was so mad I couldn't sit still. I decided to go back home and eat.

Just before I got to the house, I heard Grandma shouting. I walked up to the door of the west room where she was lying. It was slightly ajar, and I could see my mother and Im Ramzi, the woman Uncle Wadi had hired to help my mother, standing over Grandma, chattering like two excited squirrels. They were try-ing to get her to stop doing something because, they said, it was improper. They wanted her to quit before she hurt herself. I opened the door a little more to see what was happening. I saw Grandma lying on her side with her fanny exposed. She was wiping some wet brown stuff off her hand on a towel. My mother and the hired woman kept hovering and twittering. Then I heard Grandma say that it had to come out. It was poisoning her because her bowels would not move now that she was paralyzed from the waist down. She had to help herself the only way she knew how.

Grandma was very indignant, too. She was mad as I had never seen her before. And I heard her say, "This is what You do to me after all we have been through together? You forsake me in my hour of need? You let me be humiliated before my family and the whole village? Is it because I did not do right by You? Have I not fed Your ministers and given Your church aplenty? Is this how You repay me for trusting You and believing in You? And now that I am in despair, You are nowhere to be found. Where are You, You son of a bitch?"

Both Mother and Im Ramzi begged her to stop saying those things because they were blasphemous, but she did not pay any attention to them. I wanted them to let her alone. I rushed into the room to tell them to quit and leave her be, but my mother ran me off because she did not want me to see what was going on in there.

I stormed out and went to the patch where Grandma grew her fava beans (where my Dinar was buried). I filled my pockets with rocks, large and small, and started throwing them at the mountains where Grandma's God lived. I threw them as far and as hard as I could, and I called Him son of a bitch just as I had heard my Grandma do as she lay in shit and in pain on a rubber sheet on the floor of the west room. I felt righteous because my grandma and I had been wronged, and we were not going to take it lying down like the bleating sheep that Saad, the butcher, bled to death in the village square on Saturday mornings.

Throwing rocks at the Lord God and calling Him names left me exhausted. It was getting dark, too, so I went into the east room and lay down on the hard couch. I was so tired that the couch felt good. I lay there for a long time looking up at the ceiling and listening to Grandma's moans. Then, I went out like a light. But my sleep was troubled with horrible nightmares. In my dreams, Wadi, the madman who lived next door, chased me around all night and terrified me with his crazy blue eyes. Sometimes he became the God of my grandmother. I screamed and screamed in my sleep, but no sound came out of my mouth, and the people who were in my dreams: my mother, my father, and Abu Sameer, the lute player who butchered Antar, walked around me as if nothing unusual was happening. And they smiled.

The next day I woke up stiff and feeling terrible because of the nightmares and because of the things I had said and done the night before. I sat there on the edge of the couch and thought about it for a while. Then, out of the clear blue, an idea struck me like a sledgehammer, right between the eyes. All this time we have been talking to Grandma's God. Maybe He does not pay much attention to the words people speak. There are so many people and they are always saying something to Him. They want Him to do this or give them that or take care of the other thing. No wonder He is paying no attention to their words, but how many of them are *writing* to Him? How many of them are using the power of the written word to get Him to see what they want Him to see and hear what they want Him to hear? None, I bet. Not one. But that was exactly what I was going to do. I was going to write Him a letter. Now that would get His attention. Not even He could ignore the powerful magic in the written word. Right there and then, as the sun was rising from behind the Monastery of Christ the Savior, I made up my mind to write to my grandmother's God. I knew I had Him.

I looked around for a pencil and a piece of paper. I found what I needed in the chest of drawers in the east room. Then I filled my pockets with almonds and headed back to my cave.

In my cave, I lay face down on the floor, rested my paper on my story book, and got ready to write. That was when another thought, even better than the first one that had come to me earlier that morning, flashed in my head. The letter was not to be written to my grandmother's God, but to the Virgin Mary. I thought that the best way to get to God was through His son Jesus, and the surest way to get to Jesus was through His mother. He would have to do whatever His mother told him to do, as any good son would. If I could get Jesus' attention, He would get his father's, and my written petition would be heard.

The fact that I was a Presbyterian kid did not matter. Our Lady knew that I had loved her since the first day I saw her picture in the Catholic church when I sneaked in and saw Abuna Hanna, the priest, chanting in the candlelight. My mind on the task before me, I started to write.

I began my letter by telling the Virgin that I loved her. Then

I asked her to talk to her boy, Jesus, and get Him to talk to his father who lived in the hills east of our house. I begged her to tell her son that Grandma was in a lot of pain and that it was not fair to abandon her like that. I asked her to do all she could to help my Teta. I also promised her that I would try to be good and not throw rocks at God anymore. Finally, I thanked her for her kindness and wished her a long life.

I had to wait for a few minutes for the words to dry up because the pencil I used was not like any other I'd seen before. I had to lick it often to get it to write, and it tasted funny, like the milk that oozes out of fig tree bark when you cut it with a knife. It also made my tongue purple. But the good thing about that pencil was that once you wrote with it, the words could not be erased.

When the writing had dried, I folded my letter and took it to the Catholic church to deliver it to the Virgin. I squeezed in through a vent in the back of the church, facing the Presbyterian cemetery. Then I headed for the altar where I had seen my friends, dressed in white, sing to Mary during Sunday masses as Abuna Hanna swung his censor. The church was so quiet inside that the silence felt heavy on my ears. I felt as if I was underwater. But I went on to the pulpit. Carefully, I placed my letter down on the large open bible, turned around and waved at Mary, the Mother of God. I sneaked out the same way I had come in.

For the first time since Grandma had gotten that disease, I had peace. And for the next three days, Grandma just lay quietly on her mattress, without pain. Then, on the third day, her fingernails turned blue and she died.

The next day, in the afternoon, Grandma was laid to rest in the family cave in her olive grove by the village spring. Her coffin was placed between Grandpa Hassan's, who had died long before I was born, and Aunt Julia, who had burned to death before she was eighteen. I felt alone, again, the way I had when my Dinar died. Only this time it was worse because my mother was too busy with her own grief to notice what was happening to me. But I was tough like my Teta, and I could make it on my own. Besides, I had my hatred for her God to keep me going.

After the funeral I went to the house and took off my Sunday clothes. I filled my pants pockets with dried figs and almonds, packed some bread and *jibni baida* (white cheese) in a bag and quietly headed for my cave. I did not even have to be careful because nobody was paying any attention.

As I was crawling into my cave, I snagged the web of the little brown spider that shared the cave with me and tore it to shreds. I wasn't being as careful as I usually was. Frankly, I did not give a damn. The spider did not matter and neither did the little black ants that lived in the hole in the floor. I used to bring them bread crumbs and crushed wheat, and they were so happy to see me. But the day Grandma was buried I felt mean because I was only a thing made like the ants, the spider, and Abu Asaad's mules. I hated the idea that I was just a creature like them. It made me furious to think that the power was in someone else's hands, and He was immovable, refusing to do the right thing. My anger got the best of me, and I kicked the anthill and stomped the scared ants with my foot. They scurried around aimlessly, scared and confused. I sat down on the floor and looked at what I had done. Here and there I saw mangled ants trying to drag themselves back into their ruined home and dying ants that were missing legs, or antennas, lying on their backs, kicking with their feet in the air. Some were cut in half, but they still moved around, not knowing that they were dead already.

I felt ashamed because I had inflicted pain and death on the little things that caused me no harm. I realized that I was no better than my grandmother's God who lived in the hills east of our house. Like Him I showed no mercy to my little friends. But I was sorry for what I had done. And I hoped He was too.

And so, at a little over five, sitting on the floor of my cave with a homeless spider and a host of dead and dying ants all around me, I made up my mind to go it alone. Once again the lesson that I had learned when my pet, Dinar, was killed by a snake came home to me: when it came to the things that really mattered, I would always be alone.

Although I was too young to understand the impact of what had happened to me when Teta died, I know now that I lost a great mentor and friend. It was her life, not her death, that finally mattered. What she gave me in my first five years is, to this day, still shaping the life of my mind, that pyramid which I am building and ascending until I, too, become my own mountain and perhaps my own god.

9

Women

I AM ONLY fifty-five years old now, still fairly young by today's standards. I am, however, no longer interested in sex or in women. I have, as one might say, "lost it." But strange as it may seem, I am very happy with my condition and I have been reveling in it for almost a year now because it has brought me a tremendous sense of relief. Frankly, I can't remember feeling this lighthearted and free since I got "hooked" on sex when I was nine. That was when I had my first sexual experience. One thrilling encounter—that was all it took—and I fell hopelessly in love with sex.

I was a little over four when I got my first taste of the mystery, the wonder, and the joy that is woman. I was too small at the time to know exactly what I was doing or what I was feeling. All I knew was that women made me feel good. They made me feel that way all the time, but especially on those days, usually Fridays, when they came together at our house to drink Turkish coffee, talk about other women in the neighborhood, and remove the hair on their arms and legs. On those days, five, six, or seven women would get together in our west room, lock the door behind them, and start setting up for the *natf*, or the *plucking*.

Each of the women brought with her a lemon, a cup of sugar, a towel, and a pair of tweezers. They handed the sugar and lemons to my mother, who seemed to know more about it than the rest of her guests, and she would start the ritual.

First, my mother lit the Primus, a small pressurized cooking stove that burned kerosene. Then she placed a frying pan containing a little water on it. While the water was heating, she squeezed the lemons, carefully strained the juice to remove the seeds and pulp, and poured the juice into the frying pan. After that she added the sugar and stirred the mixture gently. Everything had to be just right. The ratio of the lemon juice to the sugar and the temperature of the flame had to be just right, or the *shalghini*—sticky mixture—would end up either too thin or too thick. If that happened, it would have to be thrown away and the whole operation would have to be repeated. But my mother was good at it. She knew what she was doing, and she never needed to redo her mixtures. That was probably why the neighborhood women came to our house to do their leg- and arm-hair plucking. They could not afford to make any mistakes. Lemons and sugar were not easy to come by after the Big War. Like money, those things did not grow on trees. So, there was no room for error.

Finally, when the mixture was the desired consistency, Mother took the pan off the stove and put it somewhere safe to cool. While the women waited for the *shalghini* to get cool enough to use, Mother made a big *rakwi* (coffeepot) of Turkish coffee. The women sipped their coffee and read each other's fortunes in the coffee grounds that settled in the bottom of their tiny demitasses. They talked at the top of their voices, each woman trying to speak as loudly as she could to be heard over the shouting of the other women in the room. I didn't think anybody heard or understood anything that was said. But I did not think it mattered to them, either. They were happy to be together, behind closed doors, doing *women things*, away from their men who bullied them and pushed them around all day long—from sunup till sundown—and sometimes even beyond.

When the last sip of coffee was downed and the last fortune read, the plucking began. My mother, careful to be fair, dipped into the honeylike *shalghini*, took out equal measures, and handed them to each one of the women. She took what was left for herself. Everything that stuck to the pan was mine. My mother handed me the pan and I licked it clean.

Once there wasn't enough *shalghini* left in the pan to satisfy me, so I waited for Im Bassam to put her lump down on the coffee tray beside her. When she did, I snatched it, sank my teeth into it, and took a big bite. Everybody was shocked that I would do such a thing because the lump was full of thick black hair. I didn't care. Hair or no hair, by Allah I had to have that sweet stuff, and I got it. The lump in my mouth was so big and sticky that I could not move my jaw for a while. But my spit finally did the job, and the *shalghini* eventually worked its way down to my stomach.

One of the women, Im Sami, the basket weaver's wife, told my mother that I was going to pass a hair ball the size of a duck egg, Im Bassam's legs being as hairy as they were. She told my mother to be on the look out for it.

I looked for it myself for days, but I never did see it. I didn't care. That lump of *shalghini* was worth it. It was sticky and it was sweet. But it was not the only sweet thing that I got to enjoy during those hair removal sessions. I got to watch the women and feel them, too. When they were slapping those sticky patties on their shins and calves and quickly ripping them off, they were not paying any attention to me. They were busy and they were in pain. Unnoticed, I slithered around from one woman to the next and felt the smooth, warm skin of their arms and legs. There was something very comforting about the way their bodies felt. I did not know then the words to describe what I felt, but I do now. Fondling my mother's friends had a kind of healing effect on me. It was like getting therapy. I felt warm all over. And I felt safe. Things were good. And then, a little later, they got even better.

When their shins and calves were plucked clean, the women lifted up their skirts and dresses and tied them around their waists or rolled them up under their panties to make them stay up. I loved watching them do that. Next to licking the sweet pan, the unveiling of the thighs was my second most favorite part of the whole show. In those days, Lebanese women did not reveal anything above the midcalf. Showing the knees was a no-no. Only bad (but very popular) women, like Im Kaleem, the village *shlikki* (strumpet), would do such a thing, and she was never invited to those plucking sessions at our house. I did not know why she wasn't.

The women who came to our house to pluck were just as bad and sometimes even worse than Im Kaleem. They revealed more of their hidden parts than she ever did. Take Jameeli, for example. She was in the habit of slipping out of her skirt and walking around the room half naked. I got to see her like that many times. And that was why, of all the women who came to our house, Jameeli was my favorite. She was younger than any of the other women, too. And the skin of her legs was tight, as if it were one size too small. She moved with the speed of a sleek gazelle and the muffled grace of a she-leopard. Jameeli was restless, always up and about, moving around, doing stuff. That was why I got to see more of her than any of the others. For one thing, the older women's panties were kind of baggy and they had short legs. But Jameeli's were small and tight, and I got to see shadows and suggestions of mysterious *things* through the light material they were made of. I was fascinated by the smooth curves and the firm bumps on Jameeli's body, and I got to be close to them on many occasions.

Sometimes Jameeli would take a break from the plucking and the pain. Carefully, she would lay her sticky lump on the coffee tray and then suddenly jump up and chase me around the room. And I would run and dodge her. But I did not make it too hard for her to catch me. When she finally cornered me, she would grab me under the arms and lift me up as high as she could and bring me down on her face and make farty noises on my belly and kiss me on the mouth and cheeks, and I would shriek with excitement and grab her by the hair and by the ears and by the breasts. Even today, after half a century and a whole lot of miles, I can still remember how firm her breasts felt to my touch, how warm and fresh her breath smelled and how comfortable and safe I felt when she sat me in her lap and hugged me so tightly I could not breathe.

She also used to tease me by blowing in my ears and on the back of my neck because it tickled. When she did that I had goose bumps all over me, and I wanted to feel that way all the time.

But great as Jameeli made me feel when I was four, it did not even come close to what her little sister, Wardi (Rose) made me feel five years later, in 1952, when I was nine and she was fourteen. Christ, I did not know that there was that much pleasure in the whole wide world.

In the fall of that year my father built a big concrete fireplace in the kitchen. As soon as he finished it, he tried it out. He made a big fire, and after that my poor mother had to make a lot of coffee and wash a lot of coffee cups because everybody in the village wanted to sit around our fireplace every evening of the week, including Sundays. It was on one of those cold Sunday nights in January when Jameeli's little sister opened my eyes to the mouth-drying, belly-burning type of experience that can come only with a boy's first encounter with sex.

A few of us kids were sitting on sheepskins that were piled up in the corner by the fireplace. There were quite a few of us. Yasmine, the carpenter's daughter, was there with her mama and baba. Shafeek, my wall-eyed friend, was there, too, with his sister, and Sami, the basket weaver's son. I think that Wardi was the oldest among us kids. Although she had big breasts, Wardi did not sit with the adults because she did not have a lot of hair in her armpits yet. Also, she was still playing with dolls, and she did not like drinking Turkish coffee. In Magdaluna, learning to drink and enjoy strong coffee was one of the admission tickets into the world of adults. Wardi was not there quite yet, so she had to sit with the rest of us kids. Boy, was I glad she did.

The adults, sitting on chairs around the fireplace, talked about their fields and their cows and their goats and their chickens. A double-yolked egg was a news item to be mentioned proudly at those gatherings in our kitchen. The woman whose chicken laid one of those rarities talked about it as if a new grandson had been born into her family. But the birth of a lamb was major news. Sometimes the grown-ups sang songs or listened to Ibrahim play his fiddle. And sometimes they just sat there and quietly smoked their hand-rolled cigarettes and stared into the fire. Once in a while, one of them would fall asleep in his chair and snore. His head would start to roll off his shoulders and he would suddenly wake up and wipe the drool off his chin with the back of his hand and mumble a few words that nobody understood. But most of the time our visitors were very noisy and they did not pay any attention to us kids reclining in the corner under thick, heavy blankets. That was when we got into stuff, unobserved.

It was on one of those noisy, cold nights that Wardi touched me where no girl had ever touched me before. She did it without as much as by-your-leave. I guess she knew no little boy in his right mind would object to what she had to offer.

Wardi, sure of herself and her irresistible powers, put her lips right up against my ear and whispered, "I want to touch *it*." Before my head could process what I'd just heard, her hand was between my legs and her fingers were busily probing for *it*. Then she found *it*. By that time, *it* had already gotten hard. Wardi wrapped her fingers around *it* and leaned over me and said, "My, oh, my! It is so big and hard. I like it. I really do."

When she whispered those words in my ear I got so excited that my neck got hot and my tongue swelled inside my mouth. I was afraid I was going to choke on it. But I did not care. I could have died right there and then and I would have been the happiest kid that had ever lived. I was grateful to Wardi for doing what she did to me as I had never before been grateful to anyone. And I wanted to touch her *down there*, too, only I couldn't talk. When I finally managed to get the words out, I said, "Can I put my hand, uh, *down there*, too? Please, can I? None of the other girls at school will let me do that, you know. They just won't."

Wardi did not even hesitate. She said, "Of course, you can, *Habeebi*. Here." She took my hand and stuck it between her legs. I still remember to this day the first thing that came to mind when my hand was in place. It was "Jesus, it is hot." It felt feverish, and my *thing* got even harder. The sensation went beyond pleasure. *It* began to hurt. But it was a good pain, and I wanted that feeling never to stop.

But it did. All too soon, to my chagrin. Wardi's mama and baba got up and announced they were leaving. They bid everyone good night. And they told Wardi to get her stuff together and wrap her shawl tightly around her neck and head because they did not want her to have the palsy. In those days, the village people used to believe that the shock of cold air, after being warm inside, would cause a stroke. I wanted so bad to ask them—beg them—just go down on my hands and knees and unashamedly kiss their feet and plead with them to let her stay the night. I was willing to dig their fields, empty their chamber pots, or watch their flocks of sheep in the field—*anything*—if they would let Wardi stay there with me under that blanket for the rest of the night. But, of course, I could do no such thing, and Wardi walked out of our kitchen that evening with my heart and everything else between my sternum and my knees in her hands.

10

Fear

GRANDMA'S DEATH had only confirmed to me what I had already known: *we live as we dream, alone*. Even as a kid, I knew this to be true. I learned that my fears, like my happiness and pain, had to be faced alone.

My friends and playmates had their own fears. Some of them, like Kameel, the goatherd's son, and his cousin, Habeeb, were afraid of snakes. Others, like Sami, were afraid of spiders and ghosts.

Hani, the miller's nephew, made fun of the other boys and laughed at their fears. He would catch spiders and put them in an empty soda bottle. Then when Sami showed up to play, Hani would whip the bottle out and shove it under Sami's nose. Sami would cover his eyes and run, screaming. He never seemed to learn that if you run with your hands over your eyes, you're going to bump into hard things. And that is why Sami had bumps on his head and scabs on his knees until about the time he got married.

The miller's nephew was not safe from the rest of us, though. Jirgi, the farrier's grandson (whose father died before he was even born) knew that Hani hated mice. Jirgi would catch them in the shed where his grandfather shoed horses and he would put them in a coffee can with holes in the lid. He had discovered the summer before that he had to make holes in the lid for the mice to stay alive. When we were all together in the village square, and Hani had finished terrorizing Sami, Jirgi would release the mice at Hani's feet. We all laughed as Hani, too, ran and bumped into hard things.

I did not fear any of those things. Ghosts worried me a little and snakes made me nervous, but that was about all they did. It wasn't that I was braver than any of my peers because I too knew fear well. What I dreaded was different, that was all. Only I did not let the other kids find out my secret horror. They never knew that the insane scared me out of my mind. God, how I feared crazy people. Their incoherent speech scared me, and their inscrutable doings terrified me, but what terrorized me most was their eyes, which seemed to focus intently on things that I could not see or dare to imagine. When those demented eyes fixed their gaze on mine, my backbone turned to ice. I felt like a butterfly impaled on a collector's cold steel pin. Their clutch, like hard claws, held me captive and refused, no matter how much I pleaded, to let me go.

I wasn't yet six when this fear of the insane took root in my heart and burrowed like a mole into my soul. I think where I was and when it was had a lot to do with it.

At that time, Magdaluna had none of the modern conveniences that most of the rest of the world enjoyed. Until about the end of the 1940s, we had no running water in our homes.

Electricity was unheard of, and our toilets were holes in the ground somewhere in a field far away from our homes. That was a time of flickering candles, sooty kerosene lamps, and rusty tin lanterns. It was a time when the nights were excruciatingly long because they were dimly lit and full of dancing shadows. It was a time when the dark was filled with scary noises like hooting and howling, barking and growling and the sounds of gravel and stones crunching under the huge, hard paws of foul-smelling hyenas on the prowl.

I will never forget the anguish of never being able to see clearly at night because the lights we had around the house were never bright enough to illuminate the wicked darkness for me to feel safe and secure. And there were always, always things moving about, skulking, slinking, grunting and snickering, just beyond the edge of the small circle of light that my fickle lantern or guttering candle threw so very hesitantly around me.

That was the world I lived in the first years of my childhood — a creepy world of constant goose bumps on the arms and tingling in the scalp. But what made it worse for me was that the Presbyterian cemetery was just across the gravel footpath that ran in back of our house, with only a low, broken-down, stone wall separating us from the dead and from the terror that each night, like an evil witch's cloak, brought within its folds a host of cold and unclean things.

I will remember one of those nights as long as I shall live. It was a chilly November evening. I was sitting at the kitchen table, writing my Arabic grammar homework with a quill dipped in Chinese ink. My father called my name from the east room where he was listening to his news.

"Son, I am out of cigarettes," he said. "Go over to Ibrahim's and ask him for a pack of Bafra. And tell him that I'll give him a fresh pack tomorrow as soon as I get a chance to go to the *dikkan.*"

I immediately ran out and looked to see if it had gotten dark yet. Then I thanked my lucky stars. The sun had already set, but the western sky was still blood-red with the crimson lights of another fallen autumn day. I had enough time to run to Ibrahim's and get back before it got dark enough for the dead and the jackals to come out and terrorize me.

I could have taken the gravel footpath to Ibrahim's, but to save time I decided to go over the stone wall that separated our field from his. There was a low spot in the wall by the carob tree, and I went sailing over it like a gazelle.

Ibrahim's house was dark and silent as it had been since his mother died from a stroke the past summer. There were no lights on anywhere inside, but I heard noises coming from behind the house where Ibrahim kept his beloved cow and three chickens. I walked around the hut and saw him just as he was closing the rickety wooden gate.

"Good evening, sir. My father sent me to ask you for a pack of cigarettes. He's just run out, and the store has already closed. He said he'd give you a fresh pack tomorrow."

In the dim twilight I could not see his weather-beaten face clearly, but I could hear him swallow. He always swallowed hard when he was asked for something, even when he knew he would be paid back. I could not see his eyes either, but I knew that they had narrowed down to thin slits. Ibrahim was a skinflint.

"Okay, son. Be there in a minute."

But I knew it wouldn't be a minute, or five or ten, because Ibrahim, even on warm summer days, moved like a lizard in the dead of winter. I prayed in my heart that he would hurry up so that I could get back to the safety of my home before it got too dark to see who or what the enemy was and where it was coming from to get me.

As I had feared, it took that man forever to find that pack of cigarettes. I think he looked for it in all the wrong places on purpose, hoping that I would give up and leave. But knowing how grumpy my father got without cigarettes, I decided to be brave and hang in there until Ibrahim gave in and handed me a pack of Bafra that was so old the thin cellophane wrapping on it had become brittle and crumbly.

"Thanks," I said, snatching the pack out of his gnarled hand, and bounding for the carob tree, I yelled back, "Evenin'."

It was no more than a hundred yards to the carob tree, but just before I got there, I stopped dead in my tracks because I sensed that something about the tree wasn't quite right. It was my playground, and I knew it very well. I knew the number of its branches and all the knots on them because I had spent the summer playing in it, and in the not-quite-opaque darkness, I could see that its silhouette was . . . different. At first I thought the trunk looked shorter, but then I realized that wasn't it. Actually, it looked thicker, twice as big around as I remembered it. Then it moved.

My mouth went dry and my throat closed as if it were full of dust. I wanted to run, but my knees had already turned to rubber under me. I thought of calling on Ibrahim for help but quickly abandoned that idea because whatever was lying in wait for me under the carob tree would have finished tearing me to pieces long before he got there, slow as he was. There was no point in calling my father or mother to save me either, because they were too far on the other side of the wall to hear my cry. So, like a good Presbyterian kid, I did the only thing left for me to do; I started praying Hail Mary, Mother of God, which I had secretly learned, against my father's express wishes, in Catholic summer school.

The Virgin must have heard and interceded in my behalf because God immediately responded to my prayers with a flood of silver light from a full moon that suddenly burst out into the eastern sky from behind the massive black hills in back of the Monastery of Christ the Savior. It was the biggest moon I had ever seen, as big as a school house, and in its soothing light I could see that it wasn't a beast or a ghost lurking under the old carob tree; it was only a man, a welcome mortal soul like me. But to be on the safe side, I kept up my prayers as I walked closer to the hole in the wall, my only way home.

As I got closer, I could make out that it was . . . oh, God, no, not HIM, not Wadi. My heart sank, and I wished to God that it had been a bear or a wolf, or even the ghost of a dead enemy, anything but a crazy, because I knew that I stood a better chance with a beast or a *jinni* (genie) than with this lunatic. Even if I could have run, it wouldn't have done me any good. He was in his twenties, young and athletic, with the kind of strength and speed that only crazy people like him seem to have. So, I did the only thing I knew to do when I had to manipulate grown-ups: I became very polite. I had learned this trick from Albert, my older cousin, and it almost always paid off. Only I hoped that it would work with nuts as well as it did with those who were sane. In my best controlled voice I said solicitously, "Good evening, sir. Beautiful moon tonight, isn't it?" My voice was so loud that it startled me.

He snorted, walked over to me, and grabbed me by the arm right above the elbow. His hand was soft, but cold as a snail. My heart fluttered like a bird caught in a fowler's net.

"Whose son are you?" he said, making the question sound like a lot was riding on it.

I tried hard to suppress my fear because I'd been told that dogs and madmen would attack you only if they smelled fear on you. I cleared my aching throat and said, "I am the son of Fuad, the son of Hassan, the son of Suleiman Accawi, sir."

He leaned over me and brought his face so close to mine that I could feel his tepid breath on my forehead.

"I know your father and grandfather," he said. "They're good men. Tell your father that I'm back. Tell him that I'm coming tomorrow to play him a partita (set) or two of *tawli* (backgammon). You will do that, now won't you, son of Fuad, son of Hassan?"

"Yes, sir," I replied quickly. "I sure will. Promise."

He let my arm go, and I suppressed a huge sigh of relief. I couldn't afford to let him know that he terrified me.

Once again, as he helped me over the wall, he told me to make sure to tell my father that he was coming to play him a set or two of *tawli*. And once again I swore to him that I would. As soon as I landed on the other side of the wall and there was some distance between us, my feet took over, and I *flew* home. I say *flew* because I honestly cannot remember my feet touching the ground.

I had nightmares all that night long, and I woke up soaking in cold sweat, praying to whoever would listen for help and protection from Wadi's insane blue eyes.

When I recovered a little bit from the dream, I started to reason things out in my own mind, trying to get a grip on myself. I told myself that Wadi was not the horrible creature I had made him out to be and that he was basically a harmless man. It wasn't his fault that he had been driven over the edge by a failed romance and a long run of bad luck. I also reminded myself of the many good things that my grandmother and my mother had told me about him. They said that he had been a very sweet and gentle soul before the devil entered him and took over his mind. But a woman, they said, hanging their heads and sighing in unison, came into his life and wrecked it.

Wadi was only eighteen when that happened. He was still a freshman at a Presbyterian parochial college in Sidon, and he was having a little trouble with his French that year. So Noura, the Reverend Salman's youngest daughter, offered to help him that summer because she, too, was home from college, and she thought that helping a good-looking young man with his schoolwork would only be the Christian thing to do. She was two years his senior and very beautiful. She was also given to the habit of slowly raising her skirt to massage her aching knees, which seemed to hurt and needed to be massaged whenever there were young men around.

That summer Wadi's mother died, and almost immediately after that, he fell in love with Noura head over heels. Because his father was dead too, Wadi begged his elder brother, Jaleel, to go and ask the Reverend Salman for his daughter's hand in marriage. When Noura heard about it, she rolled her large hazel brown eyes and laughed at the prospect. With a measured wave of her hand, she dismissed it as a silly notion.

That evening Wadi jumped into the forty-foot-deep cistern in the front yard of his house. He wanted to be dead.

Im Naseem, the carpenter's sister, saw him jump in as she was walking back home from our house, and she raised a shrill cry that sounded like the crack of a bullwhip in the wind. Abu George, the blacksmith, Abu Asaad, the mule skinner, and Abu Wajeeh, the gunsmith, three of the biggest and toughest men in the village, responded immediately to the cry for help. Abu George and Abu Asaad found a thick rope and let Abu Wajeeh down into the well. He wrestled with Wadi for a long time before he could get the rope around him and get him out of the well.

When Wadi was finally pulled out, eyes bloodshot and as big as saucers, he put up another fierce fight, trying desperately to throw himself back into the well. It took all three men to keep him from it and to drag him into the house.

Once inside, Wadi was instantly transformed. He stopped kicking, biting, and scratching and just sat there, wet, disheveled, defeated, and as crazy as a loon. He looked so much smaller than he had before he jumped into the well. But he was quiet now and peaceful, as if he'd gone into some secret chamber within his heart and shut the door behind him forever. He was calm, but it was an eerie calm, the kind that would make the spine of an exorcist tingle.

The village, like a swarm of green flies on a fresh turd, feasted on Wadi's story for a week, and the people in Magdaluna and the neighboring villages would have continued to suck on this scandal, embellish it, and weave more gruesome details into it, had it not been for Salam the wife of Jawdat, the village bully, who never returned anything he borrowed. Salam gave the village just what it needed, another juicy scandal, to get its mind off poor Wadi when she was caught behind Im Yussef's olive oil press in the arms of big Haseeb, the goatherd's firstborn son.

Two boys, Yohanna and Yussef, the cobbler's nephews, went behind the press to take a leak and just about fell on top of Salam and Haseeb rolling in the hay. The ruckus that ensued brought everybody at the olive press out, and the rest, well, that I leave to your imagination.

After the olive press incident, just about everybody in Magdaluna forgot about Wadi. Only my father and I didn't. We couldn't even if we had wanted to, because Jaleel, like Wadi and my father, was a serious *tawli* player, and he came over to our house regularly to challenge my father to another set, hoping that some new move that he'd picked up somewhere else, like the *dikkan*, would give him the edge against my father. During those long *tawli* games, when Wadi wasn't around, my father and Jaleel talked about his brother's *condition*. Actually, what happened was that Jaleel did the talking and my father the grunting and *uhumming* while I rolled around a ball made from old socks and eavesdropped on them.

I heard snatches of their conversation every now and then, and I started to piece together my own picture of what was happening. Wadi was not getting any better, as my father had expected. (I'd heard him many times tell Jaleel that Wadi would get better with time, the best of all healers.)

The truth was that Wadi was getting crazier. There was no doubt about it in my mind, especially after I overheard Jaleel tell my father that Wadi had been talking to himself. He complained about his brother's long rambling monologues that kept him awake most of the night. He also said that Wadi had gotten into the habit of washing his hands and ears frequently and that he'd been asking for a walking stick.

That really whet my curiosity. "Why in the world," I asked myself, "would a crazy but healthy young man like Wadi need a cane?" God, how I loved a mystery.

Three or maybe four days later, the mystery began to unravel.

It was late in the afternoon, and I was going to Abu Fareed's store to buy a bottle of *Kazouza* (soda), with fifteen copper piasters strung on a shoelace around my neck. When I went around the corner of Ibrahim's house, I came up suddenly on Wadi pissing against the stone wall between the one-room school-house and Ibrahim's cottage. I ducked immediately and waited for a few moments. Nothing happened. I was relieved because my presence hadn't been detected. Then, very carefully, I took a peek. Wadi was buttoning up his pants.

When he finished, he grabbed his cane, which his brother had gotten him just to shut him up, I suppose, and started to wag it to this side and that at something or someone that only he could see. I think he was trying to get it to move because I heard him say, "Move before you get your feet wet."

The hair on my head moved like the spikes on a hedgehog. This was getting to me. But, terrified as I was, I could not turn around and run. Like a sparrow in the bush, I was *snaked* by what was happening right before my eyes. Then, Wadi started on one of his monologues that I'd heard Jaleel tell my father about. But this wasn't a monologue; it was a dialogue! Wadi was arguing with someone, not just talking to himself. It seemed that whoever or whatever he was talking to was angry about something. Oh, he was mad and he was telling Wadi about it because Wadi had been thinking some foolish thoughts; he'd been thinking about forgiving Noura and getting on with his life. But Wadi's *familiar* (as my grandmother called things unseen) did not go for this forgiveness thing, and he was giving Wadi a piece of his mind. Wadi tried to defend himself vehemently, and for a moment I thought he was going to strike his *companion* with his cane, but he must have backed off quickly. Wadi slowly returned his walking stick to his side, and muttering to himself, walked into the Presbyterian cemetery and disappeared.

As soon as it was safe to come out, I slithered back to the house. He never found out that I had seen him. I would have known if he had.

My third encounter with Wadi came about a week later. I was going to Im Sameer's to play with my friend Rafeek, Im Sameer's youngest son, who was about my age. To get to her house, I had to go by Wadi's house, which sat on a slope that put the window of Wadi's room at just about my eye level. As I walked by, I heard a racket coming from Wadi's room. Naturally, I stopped to investigate. Wadi's back was turned to me, and I got to watch, undetected, what was going on.

Again, Wadi was having an argument with someone, but this time it couldn't have been the same *thing* I had seen him contend with before. This was a big one because Wadi, a tall man himself, was looking up at him. Wadi turned a little to his left and started yelling at another fellow. This had to be the *familiar* that I had seen him threaten with his stick by the schoolhouse. He was having a time keeping up with those two, and then more of them joined in. Wadi started shaking his cane at what seemed to be a roomful of invisible creatures all around him. There had to be a legion of them, and he was definitely losing the argument because I saw him fling his cane at them angrily and throw himself on his bed with his hands over his ears, screaming, "Yes, yes. I will, I will. You can't stop me," and he sobbed, his face buried in his pillow.

I felt sorry for Wadi that day, but I also hated him more than ever before because he scared me. So, whenever he came to play *tawli* with my father I stayed away. But there were times when I had to go into the east room, and that was when I overheard Wadi and my father talk, really talk, about politics and hunting and books, of all things, books! Wadi, it seemed, liked somebody called Mark Train or Dwain, and he talked a lot about him and some other writer from France or Anatole or someplace like that. He also must have known some very good jokes because he made my father laugh and laugh until he almost fell off his chair.

Sometimes I wondered if my father knew how crazy Wadi was. I also thought that maybe he liked him because his name was Wadi, like my uncle's. I don't know. Grown-ups just didn't make much sense to me most of the time. They didn't seem to notice how terrible things around them were either, or maybe they just didn't care. I mean, my father had to be blind not to have noticed, during those long *tawli* games, how Wadi kept swatting at his invisible companions who were hiding right there under the table. I guess he thought that Wadi was shooing away flies or something.

To his brother's chagrin, Wadi occasionally beat my father at his game, but my father did not mind. He seemed to enjoy playing with Wadi more than with Jaleel, his sane brother. I think my father believed that Wadi's condition was only a passing thing because I heard him and my mother talk about it one evening. They did not know I was listening in on their conversation, and I heard my father say, "You know, Nazira, I think Wadi would get better if he got married. All he needs is a good woman to make him feel normal again." My mother did not agree with my father because, she said, marriage might do exactly the opposite. And who would marry a crazy man, she added, on the outside chance that he might get well? Sex, she pronounced with conviction, was not the best of all therapies, as my father had often told her, and neither was it a cure for insanity. Her comment was not well received by my father, who only grunted in response and said nothing, or maybe he did, but I did not hear anything after that. I must have drifted off to sleep.

That night Wadi did not come to me in my dreams.

As the days went by, I began to see some changes in him. He looked different, but I couldn't quite put my finger on it. Nobody else seemed to notice. Only I did, because he scared me, and I studied my fear carefully. At first I thought his eyebrows were getting bushier, but then I realized that it wasn't his eyebrows that were changing but his brow ridges. They stuck out a little more than they used to. Or maybe it was his pale blue eyes that had sunk deeper into their sockets that made his brow ridges jut out the way they did. His back wasn't as straight as a rod anymore, and he placed his feet flat on the ground as he trudged around. The spring had gone out of his walk and his skin, especially the skin on his face, his ears, and the back of his hands, had gotten thin and shiny. It looked like rice paper, brittle and easy to tear. Wadi was beginning to look on the outside the way I imagined he was on the inside.

Each day he seemed to develop more and more irritating habits. He started to blow his nose all the time and his nose stayed red and swollen. He also started to wear his belt tight at first. Then he gave up wearing a belt altogether and took to wrapping a rope around his waist. He wrapped that rope so tightly that I found it hard to breathe when I looked at him. He also continually checked the rope with his nervous, pale fingers to make sure it was still there, holding his pants up. When he was not washing his hands or shooing his demons with his cane, he was blowing his nose or checking the rope around his obscenely thin waist. God, how I hated him.

My fear of Wadi became so intolerable that I couldn't take it anymore. I wished him dead. It bothered me a lot to feel about him the way I did because it was evil, only I could not help myself. I was just a kid, but I knew why I hated him and wanted him dead or gone to where I did not have to look at him anymore. He threatened everything I knew and loved. He was a constant reminder that I was fragile, that all of us—my father, my mother, my sisters, and I, everybody—was breakable, and I wanted to be rid of him and his insane blue eyes that haunted me, waking and sleeping.

I did not expect it to happen as quickly as it did, but I got half my wish about six months later, when Wadi's brother had him committed to an insane asylum called *Asfourieh (Bird House)*, which was not a real hospital in any sense of the word. It was more like a prison for the mentally disturbed, a hell from which no patient ever left, except feet first. My grandmother called it the tombs.

About a year and a half later, I got the second half of my wish. Wadi fell to his death from a third story window, trying to escape from the asylum. His brother was told that Wadi had died instantly, and he assured us, as he himself was assured by the hospital official in the grimy red fez, that Wadi did not suffer at all and that we all should take great comfort in that.

Well, I didn't. Jesus, how I hated that messenger and myself when I heard the news. True, I was finally rid of Wadi and his crazy blue eyes, and I should have been relieved at his death, but I wasn't. Something inside me, something not quite definable but very delicate and fresh, was crushed when Wadi died. He took that part of me with him to wherever mad people go when they die. I couldn't quite understand how his death affected me. All I knew was that when Wadi died I couldn't be me anymore.

His death, like my grandmother's, stirred within me conflicting feelings about God and being human. But crazy as it may sound, there are times when I miss the bastard.

My memory of Wadi has dimmed with the passing of the years, but I can still remember how his skinny knuckles looked when he wrapped his hand around the smooth handle of his cane. I remember his shiny, well-scrubbed face and his long, narrow feet. He wore tan shoes with black patches over the little toes. I remember.

But it is Wadi's voice and his eyes, which remain more real in my memory than even those of Abu George, whom I loved. The madness that I saw in Wadi's eyes and the insanity that I heard in his voice would continue to haunt me for the rest of my days. I hear Wadi's voice every time I get an anonymous call in the middle of the night because somebody in the Arab world has done wrong. When the American embassy in Beirut was blown up by terrorists, when the marines were butchered by a suicide bomber as they slept in their barracks in Beirut, and when the United States went to war with Iraq, the phone calls came non-stop, night after night.

"Go back to wherever you came from, boy. We don't want you here, you hear?" the voices would say. And "It was your people who killed *our* marines." I heard Wadi's voice on the street corner and at the laundromat when someone would murmur "sand nigger" or "camel jockey" or "rag head" under his breath, then wrinkle his nose and walk away. And I saw Wadi's eyes, too. I saw them in the face of the man who stalked me for four days in the summer of 1972, when I came back from Lebanon to see my in-laws in the States. That was when eleven Israeli athletes were massacred at the Munich summer Olympic Games. The man said nothing to me. He just followed me around in his beat-up Chevy. But on the last day he pointed his index finger at me and twitched his thumb, simulating a gun hammer falling, and sped away never to return again. But that was not the last time I would see Wadi's crazy eyes. I still see them every day in the faces of men and women on the street, on TV, in church, and in the office. And they still scare me as much as they ever did. This fear of the insane is something that I have not yet out-grown. Sometimes I wonder if I ever will.

11

Ice

The summer I turned seven, I made two important discoveries. The first one was ice. The second was a safe way to keep my treasure—a handful of copper coins—from being lost or stolen. I had amassed my small fortune running errands for my father and his drinking buddies. When my father and his friends got together to play cards or trick track, sometimes they would run out of cigarettes or *arrack*, and they would send me to the village store for a pack of this or a bottle of that. I did not mind running those errands for them because I got to keep the change, which was never much. My father and his friends would always figure what the drinks or smokes cost and give me just enough money to buy what they needed. But I watched my piasters and managed over a period of weeks to stash away enough change to treat myself every now and then to a soda or to some rock candy, which I bought at Abu Fareed's *dikkan*.

I liked Abu Fareed, the store keeper, because he was never in a hurry, and he always took the time to talk to me. He would ask me how I was doing in school or if I had been doing any hunting with my father. I liked being asked about hunting because it made me feel grown up. The truth was that I did not *hunt* with my father. I was more like his retriever. He would shoot the quail or partridges, and I would run into the bushes or tall grass and locate the fallen birds and bring them back to him. Sometimes I wondered if Abu Fareed knew. If he did, he never said anything to me about it, and I liked him for that. But what I liked about him most was that he always gave me more than my money's worth. He lost on every sale he made to me. Sometimes I suspected that he was kind to me because I helped him during olive oil season. I couldn't be sure why Abu Fareed chose to be good to me, but I was glad he was, and I would always remember him for being a friend and for what he did for me that summer in 1949.

One muggy August afternoon, while everybody in the house was having their siesta, I had an irresistible urge for one of Abu Fareed's sodas, which he kept in a bucket at the bottom of the deep well behind his store. I put on my sandals and walked down from our house on the hill to Abu Fareed's store by the threshing floor with my necklace of coins hanging around my neck. It was so hot that even the dogs were off the streets.

As I walked through the village, I thought about sodas and how much pleasure they had been to me since Abu Fareed had started selling them the summer before. I thought about how they looked and smelled and tasted and how they should be drunk to get the most out of them. I had learned that the secret to enjoying a soda is never to drink it in a hurry. You have to take your time because every step of the ritual is important. First, you watch carefully as Abu Fareed flips the lid off the top of the bottle with his opener. Then you listen to the bottle hiss. You don't want to be talking then, because you don't want to miss that sound. It is a good sound; it tickles the ears like a feather. After that, you watch the magic bubbles that suddenly appear from nowhere slowly rise up the narrow neck of the bottle, and you wonder every time if they are going to make it all the way up to the top and, once they do, if they are going to spill out. If they look like they are going to, Abu Fareed hands you the bottle quickly so you have time to slurp off the foam just before it runs down the side of the bottle and drips on the dirt floor. You have to be careful not to slurp too fast, though, because sometimes, when you take in too much fizz all at once, the soda will come out your nose and you will choke and cough and get the hiccups. You will have to breathe your own stale breath over and over again from a brown paper bag. If that does not work (and it hardly ever does), you have to eat a lot of sugar or ask a friend to pull your ears or startle you to make the hiccups go away.

Now, after you've taken your first sip and everything is under control again, you lift up the bottle against the sun and you look at it long and hard, and you wonder what they've put in it to make it taste so good. You try to guess what this secret ingredient is that makes your tongue, the gums around your teeth, and your throat tingle like that. Sometimes, on a quiet day, you can even hear the bubbles in your mouth murmuring in your ears. It's a funny sound that comes from the inside of your head.

Another thing to keep in mind when drinking a soda is not to take too long to finish it, especially on hot summer days, because it will go flat, and then it will taste like wet sugar and baking soda mixed, which leaves an awful taste on the tongue. I made that mistake once, only once. When it came to getting the most out of a soda I was somewhat of an expert, and that day I was going to enjoy it twice as much, considering how hot it was.

Suddenly I found myself at the door of Abu Fareed's store. I stepped in. It was cool and dark inside, but the store looked deserted. There was nobody behind the counter. I listened for some sound from the back of the store, but there was none. I walked to the back, where Abu Fareed took his siesta in the afternoon on hot days. He was there just as I had expected. He was lying on a cot made from the lumber of shipping crates. He heard my footsteps and sat up on the edge of the cot, rubbing his eyes and yawning.

I said, "Good day to you, Abu Fareed."

He said, "And to you, too, Anwar, son of Fuad. What in the world are you doing out in this heat? It's hot enough out there to boil the brains inside your head. And you're not even wearing a hat. What is it that brings you here on a day like this?"

I said, "I've come for a soda. It's hot, and I've got to have one. Could you get me one, please?"

"Well, well, let's see now. If I remember right, it's *Kakula* (Coca Cola) you like, isn't it?" he asked. I nodded and waited for him to go get my soda from the well behind the store. But he didn't. He got up and walked toward the sagging wooden counter by the front door. I didn't know what he was up to. I was sure that he understood me, but he was headed in the wrong direction. I was just about to say something to him about it when he reached for a heavy burlap bag covering a box that stood beside the counter. When he removed the bag, I saw that underneath it there was a box the size of a storage chest. It was painted light blue and it stood high off the floor on four slender legs. I had never seen that box before.

Abu Fareed opened the lid of the box and reached down into it. He fumbled around in there, looking for my drink. I heard the familiar tinkling and clanking of soda bottles knocking against each other. It was a delightful sound. But I wondered why Abu Fareed was keeping his drinks in the store instead of the well the way he usually did. It didn't make sense. The well was much cooler than the inside of the store. One thing was certain, though. I wasn't going to pay Abu Fareed for a warm soda. It wasn't fair. I had walked quite a stretch in the heat, and for what? A lukewarm soda? I would not have it.

Abu Fareed interrupted my thoughts. He turned around with a soda bottle in his left hand. He tapped the countertop with his finger, indicating where he wanted me to lay my money. He wanted his fifteen piasters. I took my necklace of piasters from around my neck, untied the ends of the shoelace, and carefully counted out fifteen piasters. Abu Fareed watched me count them out. He waited until I put the money down to tell me that my money was worthless.

He said, "I hate to tell you this, son, but your money is no good. All these piasters of yours can't buy you a stick of gum now. They aren't worth anything anymore." When I heard Abu Fareed say that, I did not believe him. I looked up at his face to see the twinkle in his eyes, the joke behind them. He had pulled my leg like that once or twice before, and I thought he was doing it again, but he looked serious. What he told me was meaningless, and I said, "What do you mean, my money is no good? How can money stop being good? Wasn't it just last week that you sold me some Damascus chewing gum? You took my ten piasters then. Don't you remember? You do, don't you?"

"That was last week," he said, rubbing his nose. "Your money is no good now because the government in Beirut has discontinued these copper coins. They've issued paper money to replace them. Didn't you know that? Everybody in the village knows. I'm sure your father does too. They've been announcing it in church for weeks."

Abu Fareed was telling the truth. I heard it in his voice. I saw it in his eyes, and I was crushed. I did not know what to say. But I still could not understand how money could stop being good. And I wondered who was this government in Beirut that said money could or couldn't buy stuff. A hive of mixed feelings, like angry hornets, began to buzz around inside my chest when I realized that I was poor. I felt angry and humiliated. Being penniless made me feel worthless and, worst of all, stupid. My face got hot and my lower lip began to twitch. I felt lightheaded, and I had to sit down.

Abu Fareed was still standing by his new box with the wet soda in his hand. The bottle looked cold, and it was sweating big drops that ran down its side and dripped on the counter. But it wasn't my soda anymore. It could never be mine now because I had no money. It looked so ugly then, and I hated the very sight of it. Abu Fareed's voice called me back from the pit of despair, where I was going down, down, around and around. He was moving toward me, his hand stretched out as if he was offering me the drink. He was saying, "Hey, kid, are you all right? You don't look so good. You're not going to be sick here in my store, are you, boy? Here, take this. Drink it down. It'll make you feel better. Take it."

"But my money is no good. I can't pay you for it." I said, feeling great shame.

"Don't you worry about that. I'll get my money later. Just don't you worry about it now, you hear?" He took my hand and wrapped my fingers around the neck of the soda bottle. It was so cold that I was shocked when I grabbed it. I had never handled anything that cold in my whole life. I didn't know that it was possible for anything to be that cold. I thanked Abu Fareed for the drink and asked him, "How did you do that? How did you make the bottle so cold?"

He said, "I guess you didn't know. I've got me an icebox now. I got it day before yesterday. Abu Asaad brought it up from Sidon on the back of his mule." I said, "What was that again? What did you say it was called?"

"An icebox. It's called an icebox. Don't you know what an icebox is?" he asked.

I told him I didn't. I told him that I had never heard of ice before this. I didn't know what it was or what it looked like. Abu Fareed was surprised that I had never seen ice, and he asked me, "Would you like to see it now? You want a piece of ice, son?" I said, yes.

Shaking his head, Abu Fareed walked to the icebox and lifted the lid. He took something that looked like a shoemaker's awl and started stabbing the thing called ice with it. He did that repeatedly, as if he was trying to kill it. Then he reached into the box and brought out a chunk of wet, clear glass. He walked back to me and said, "Open your hand." I did, and he placed the chunk of glass in my palm. It was even colder than the soda bottle. It was so cold it stung. I had to put my soda down and move the chunk of glass from one hand to the other to keep it from *burning* my fingers. "What is this thing, Abu Fareed? What is it, and how did you make it so cold?" I asked.

"It's what I have been telling you, ice," he said. "I didn't make it myself; I bought it. They make ice like that in Sidon. I had Abu Asaad bring me a couple of blocks."

"Well, what is it? What's it made of? Do you know?" I asked.

"It's water. That's all it is, just plain good old water." He answered.

Once again I looked up at Abu Fareed's face to see the joke, but he wasn't kidding. He was dead serious, and I said, "What do you mean, it's water? How could it be water? It's hard, like a rock."

He said, "That's what happens when water gets very cold; it freezes solid like that. But in this heat, it won't stay that way very long, you know. It will melt. It'll go back to being water again."

Abu Fareed was right. That chunk of solid water in my hand began to melt just as he said it would. Right before my eyes, it was changing back to water and dripping off my fingers onto the floor. When I realized what was happening, I panicked. I did not want my piece of ice to melt away and be lost forever. I said to

Abu Fareed, "Is there anything you can do to stop it from melting away? I want to keep it. Can you stop it, please?"

Abu Fareed said no. No one could stop ice from melting. But it could be slowed down. He told me that he wrapped a burlap bag around his blocks of ice to make them last, but there was nothing he could do to keep them from melting away eventually. Nothing. Then he asked me if I had a handkerchief. I told him I did. He said that if I wrapped the chunk of ice in it, I would get to keep it longer. So I took my handkerchief out of my pocket and carefully wrapped my precious piece of ice in it. But in no time at all, my handkerchief was soaking wet. My chunk of frozen water was getting smaller and smaller by the minute. And the tighter I held it the faster it melted. Then it came to me to put it in my pocket to keep it from melting so fast, but it got smaller faster. I took it out and looked at it. It wasn't even half the size it was when Abu Fareed handed it to me. I felt powerless and began to despair. There was nothing I could do to keep my piece of ice from vanishing completely. Within minutes it was gone. Not a trace of it was left, not even a sliver, and I felt miserable.

But my first encounter with that magical hunk of solid water Abu Fareed gave me would later become a constant reminder to me of how fleeting everything around me is, and that has helped me to appreciate what I have at the moment. Because of that melting chunk of ice I have learned to be here, now.

12

The Olive Press

MANY CHARACTERS in the village helped shape my life and mold it into what it is today. Good and bad, they have their place in my life and in my pyramid. This day I find myself standing in 1950, the fourth tier. I look around me at all the beautiful stones I have crafted for every one of these men and women. I remember them all, their names and faces, as if no time has passed at all since I lived among them more than forty years ago. To me the past is not something left behind, like smoke trailing a locomotive. It is more like little chambers hidden, like Easter eggs, here and there in the present. And I can walk into any one of these chambers any time I please. Today, for example, I am not *remembering* that first day in Elul (September) in 1950. I *am standing* in it, and I am thrilled. It is not a holiday, however. Nobody is getting married or christened or circumcised in the village today. It is not my birthday either. I've already had that earlier in the summer, on June 15, when I turned eight.

There is really nothing much going on in Magdaluna today. All the summer shows are over. The Gypsies have already come and gone. So have the Turk and his big Russian bear, and the tinner and his little brown boy. The Moroccan medicine man, riding his gleaming black horse with the red tassels and blue beads, is not due yet. It's too early in the month. He will show up with his saddle bags full of ointments and roots, tree bark, and potions later, toward the end of September, just before the first autumn shower falls. Then summer will be officially over.

But quiet and uneventful as it is, this is one of my favorite days of the year, and I am as excited about it as Stella, the mayor's hound dog, gets before a partridge hunt. Today Im Yussef's olive oil press opens after being idle and silent for nearly ten months.

I get up at dawn, before anybody else in the house stirs. I put my clothes and my sandals on and walk into the kitchen. I go straight to the large clay tub where the wheat tortillas are kept. I take three pieces, roll them up in a clean kitchen rag, and stick them under my arm. The sun is not up yet when I walk out the gate. I turn left and walk in back of the house. The wall of the Presbyterian cemetery is on my right now. Just past it is the lute player's house. His name is Abu Sameer. He's the one that bought Antar the raccoon from the old man, and then he took it home and killed it and ate it. But that was a long time ago, when I was five.

There is a sweet smell in the air. It's coming from Abu Sameer's rose garden. Abu Sameer's house is surrounded by rose bushes that seem always to be in bloom: red and yellow and white roses the size of plates. All around his house there are fruit trees, too, lots of them: pear and apricot and fig trees, everywhere. Abu Sameer spends a lot of his time tending his rose garden and his fruit orchard. He is constantly watering, weeding, and digging around his plants. He even talks to them and sings to them. My mother says that the sun has finally gotten to him and cooked his brains. She says that anyone who spends as much time in the summer sun as Abu Sameer does is a fool. He doesn't even wear a pith helmet or a straw hat. He covers his head with a thin cotton handkerchief that has four knots tied, one in each corner.

Abu Sameer seems to be gentle and harmless all right, but he's got to be crazy, like my mama says he is, to do the things he does sometimes. I don't think he's all crazy, though, like Wadi, the blue-eyed mad man who lived next door; just some part of Abu Sameer is whacko; one small section in his brain must be off because sometimes he just doesn't make sense. How can a man who loves roses as much as he does butcher a pet raccoon and eat it? How can a man who plays the lute so well and sing so sweetly turn around and whip his little girl with a switch until her calves turn black and blue? I've seen him beat her until the welts on her legs oozed a sticky yellowish stuff, like almond tree gum.

I don't understand the man, and I have never liked him. Frankly, I wouldn't miss him if he were dead or gone. He almost was the summer before when he picked a juicy pear from one of his trees and took a bite. I watched him from behind the wall of the cemetery. He coughed a little and for a moment stood still. Then he started turning red and his eyes bugged out. He clutched the collar of his shirt tightly with both hands and started running around in the field like a dying rooster. I have seen roosters many times do that after Grandma Mariam slit their throats. She would hold a bird firmly between her knees, grab it by the comb, and pull its head back. Then she would make one long pass with her sharp kitchen knife. When she released them, they would flop around wildly.

That day I saw the same thing happening to Abu Sameer. He staggered around in his field like one of those rooster. He fell down a few times and got up to run some more. Then he tripped on a small bush. He pitched forward and his chest struck a tree stump hard, and out flew a big white chunk of pear. He drew his breath in and filled his lungs with fresh air. He sounded like a full balloon when you pinch its neck as you let the air out. It squeals. That was the sound I heard Abu Sameer make when he started breathing again. After his color returned, he got up and looked around to see if anybody had been watching. He did not see me behind the cemetery wall. He dusted his clothes, tucked his shirttail into his pants and smoothed his gray hair back with his hands. Then he staggered back to his house.

But today is the first day of September, and I am not going to let my thoughts about Abu Sameer spoil it for me. I put him and his madness out of my mind. I am on my way to Im Yussef's olive press, where the oil will flow fresh and thick and green and its sweet smell will fill the whole village.

Now I am walking down the old steps between our house and the Mussa's. Wadi used to live there before he went crazy and had to be sent to the insane asylum. As I walk by the gate, I see the mouth of the well into which Wadi jumped to drown himself shortly after Noura turned down his proposal of marriage. I feel a chill running down my spine as I walk by the gate, and I pick up my steps.

Just beyond Jaleel's house on my left is Magdaluna's cactus patch. It's huge, the size of our school yard. That is the cactus patch I fell in when I was six. God, I can't believe how stupid I was when I was six. One day, for no reason at all, I got up on the stone wall above the cactus and tried to walk it from end to end. Somewhere in the middle of the wall, I stepped on a loose stone and plunged into a green sea full of thorns. When my mother and Abu Bassam, our neighbor, pulled me out, I looked like a hedgehog. There were thorns everywhere. I had to lie down on my my stomach forever until my mother finished removing the last of the thorns from my buns. She had to do it with her eyebrow tweezers, one thorn at a time.

I walk another fifty yards until I reach the fork in the road just before Abu George's house. I take the left fork. This one goes to the olive press. The right one goes to the village spring, which is in a ravine about a mile farther down the road. That is where the whole village gets its drinking water. Every day my mother carries a clay jar down to the spring and carries it back full, on her head, all the way up to our house on top of the hill. She usually does that before I wake up in the morning. The water from that spring is cold and sweet. My mother says it is tastier than grapes and figs, especially in the month of *Tashreen* (October). On warm summer days, my friends and I go down there to stick our feet in the long trough where the shepherds and goatherds, like my friend Kameel and his cousins, water their flocks every afternoon.

The village spring is also a great place to have a picnic. When my friends and I go there we do not need to take any water or food with us. There is always plenty to eat in the fields around the spring: grapes, figs, apricots, and pomegranates. Sometimes there are cucumbers, tomatoes, and corn. The rules are simple. You are welcome to eat your fill of anything that you find in the fields as long as you do not carry any of it away. If you do, that would be stealing—a great shame. I might go down there later today and wade in the cool water and wait for Kameel and his cousins to come with their flocks.

We might play a game of mumblety-peg in the mud by the trough or just sit around in the shade and chew on straws and talk and watch the baby goats at play or the big he-goats butt heads. Those big billy goats of Kameel's put on a show for us every now and then, especially in rutting season. The best fights were always between males that were evenly matched in size and weight. Two of them would rise up on their hind legs, towering over the rest of the flock. They would pause for a second at their full height, then come down like landslides, swift, massive, and unstoppable. When their foreheads made contact there was a loud, bone-shattering boom. The ravine echoed it back to us again and again, and my head hurt. But that was then and I am here now, and I have other things on my mind this morning. I am on my way to the old olive press, because today is the first day of the September and the olives are coming in ripe and shiny and full of juice. I walk on.

Just past the fork in the road stands, like a citadel, the house of Abu George, the farrier. It is on my right. I can smell it long before I get to it. It smells of iron and horse sweat and burnt coal. This is how Abu George smells too. He smells just like his house does. And I love it. I love him too, although he keeps calling me the son of the Turkish one. Every time I walk by or stop to watch him at work, he will say to me, "How is the son of the Turkish one today?" And I pretend to be impatient with him and say, "My mother is not Turkish. Why can't you get it straight? She is Syrian, okay? Syrian. They are not the same." And he always says the same thing back to me, "Turkish, Syrian, what the hell is the difference as long as she can cook."

Abu George loves his food, and he is big. He is a head taller than any other man in Magdaluna, including his cousin Abu Asaad, the mule skinner. He has a long white beard and a headful of thick white hair. His shoulders are broad and powerful and his chest is huge. He has to have the biggest pair of lungs in the whole world. His voice is every bit as big as his body. When he laughs or shouts greetings at passersby you feel the vibrations in your chest and arms. If there is a funeral or a wedding in the village, Abu George stands on the flat roof of his house and shouts the news to the neighboring villages, and they hear him miles and miles away. Even the Gypsies. If it's a funeral they come to mourn and eat well, and if it's a wedding they come to beat their drums and dance and eat well.

I ate well too, every time I stopped by to watch Abu George making horseshoes and nailing them to the hoofs of large horses and mules. He would say to me, "The wife has made some tasty date-filled cookies. Want some?" He never paid any attention to my answer. Whether I said yes or no to his offer, it was always the same. He would look back over his shoulder toward his house and call to Rahmi, his wife, "The son of the Turkish one is here. You still have any of those cookies left?"

Rahmi could not pretend that she didn't hear him. But she would take her time. And he would have to holler again. Then she would show up with a blue plate covered with a clean white pillowcase. Without saying a word, she would set the plate down on a tree stump before us and turn around and go back into the dark recesses of her house. I had to eat fast when I was around Abu George. To him it was one cookie, one bite, and the plate was wiped clean in minutes. He was unbelievable. He could be putting metal bands on a wooden barrel, straightening up a wheel axle, or pounding away on a red-hot horseshoe and still outeat me every time.

But he was a pleasure to watch, whether he was eating date-filled cookies, smoking his tiny clay pipe, or hammering smoking steel. He seemed to move in step with the world around him, as if he could hear the drummer to whose beat the seasons, the wind, and the stars moved. He was a man at home, and when I was around him I felt at home too. There was music in everything he did — his life, his laugh, his work. His heavy hammer came down on a horseshoe, one, two, three, then on the anvil, one, two. And again, one, two, three, one, two. Sparks flew off in every direction when his hammer struck glowing iron.

Sometimes when I was watching him at work, I could not help but wonder why Jesus had not chosen to be a blacksmith like Abu George instead of being a wimpy little carpenter like Abu Bassam. Isn't blacksmithing more like what God does anyway? A carpenter works with wood, a light and perishable stuff, and he hardly ever uses a sledgehammer or fire in his work. How unlike a god a carpenter is. No, Jesus should have been a blacksmith. That would have been a more befitting profession.

Abu George would have made a good god himself. His joy, his laugh, his beard, his big pot belly, and his powerful shoulders would have qualified him for the job. He was generous, too. He loved to give what he had and he always gave his very best. He was truly a mountain like my grandmother had said he was. She used to tell me that when you are excellent, you become a mountain, like Abu George. And others will see you for what you are and they will come seeking after you. She was right.

Men, rich and powerful men, honored him and showed him respect because they recognized his workmanship and his excellence. They came to him from far and wide to ask him—to beg him—to shoe their animals—Arabian horses that cost more than a field or a house. And they would humbly stand and wait while he did his magic. Even the proud horses that had thunder in their necks and breathed smoke out of their huge nostrils quieted down at his touch. They would not stand still for anyone else, but when Abu George laid his hand on their necks and whispered in their pricked ears, they relaxed and their ears lay down. They stood still as he held their feet firmly between his knees and pulled the old nails out of their hoofs. They did not budge even when he shaved off layer after layer of marbled hoof. Only after he finished nailing the new shoes on and snipping off the nail tips did they dance around and shake their manes and neigh. They stomped the ground mightily with their newly shod hoofs and trotted around the yard surefooted and at ease, as if to show their pleasure and satisfaction with a job well done.

It still is too early in the morning even for Abu George to be up and about. But maybe on the way back home I'll stop and see him today. I might even bring him a loaf of my bread soaked in fresh oil. I don't know yet. I'll see. I move on down the rocky footpath, leaving Abu George's house behind me. But the smell of it stays with me. It's inside my head. There will never come a time when it won't be there.

Now Abu Ameer's house is coming into view. It is slightly to the north-east of Abu George's. It is a tiny little house. Its door is so low that even I have to bow my head down to get in. The windows are small too, making the house look mean, just like the little man who lives in it. The village calls Abu Ameer the tinkerer and snitch because he is constantly messing with things that have cogs and wheels and springs, and he is always complaining to the government about everybody. I have been to his house many times. When our Primus kerosene stove needs a new head or our tin oil lamp springs a leak, my mama sends me to Abu Ameer's to have it fixed. He solders the cracks and holes and stops the leaks. He replaces firing pins on hunting rifles too when they wear out. He does good work, but nobody likes him because he tells on them.

When the gendarmes in their immaculate khaki riding pants and long, shiny black boots come riding into the village with their Martini rifles slung over their shoulders, Abu Ameer runs to greet them and tell them who has been doing what. He offers to feed the tall, lean men and water their frothing red horses, but they turn him down. Even they don't like him because they know that he is a rat. I don't like him, not only because he is a snitch but because he has made a fool of me and stolen from me many times before.

I walk on to the large flat stone in the middle of the village square, where Saad, the Moslem butcher, kills one of his fat-tailed sheep every Saturday morning and hangs it from a branch of the old carob tree.

Saad is not from Magdaluna. His home is in a small village somewhere in the east in the mountains of Joun. He makes his living by walking around from village to village with a small flock of sheep that gets smaller and smaller with every stop he makes. He travels like grim death, leaving behind him a trail of sheep horns and skins and bones. He always does his business before sunup, under the cover of darkness, before anybody is up. By sunrise his lamb is skinned and dressed and ready to carve and sell in kilos, half kilos, and uqqas (ounces) to the women who come like worshipers at an evil pagan rite. But they do not come to make offerings; they come to take quivering flesh in large plates and baskets that they carry in their calloused hands. They have to get up early to get the meat they want, because by nine o'clock the best parts of the lamb are gone. Only the poorest folk in the village wait until then to carry away, like vultures, what is left: the guts, the feet, and the head.

One Saturday morning last summer, my mother woke me at dawn. It was still fairly dark outside. She said that she wanted to be there this morning before any of the other women got to Saad and his meat. She asked me if I was interested in going with her to see what Saad did. I said yes. I had seen Grandma kill chickens many times, but I had never seen anybody slaughter a sheep. My curiosity got the best of me. I wanted to know what it was like. So, I hurriedly put on my clothes and my sandals and followed her down to the *saha* (village square) below our house.

When my mama and I got there, there was nobody around. Only Saad and his small flock of sheep were standing in a grassy patch off to the side of the road. Saad looked like Jesus in the pictures I had seen on the walls of the Catholic church behind the Presbyterian cemetery. But Saad did not have a shepherd's crook in his hand as Jesus did. He had a piece of rope wrapped, like a serpent, around his wrist. His sheep walked around him, chomping on the little clumps of grass they found here and there at his feet. They looked so peaceful in the quiet cool of the morning mist. They had no idea that one of them would end up in our stomachs before the sun reached high noon. I felt a little uneasy in my chest, but I was curious. I did not know what to expect, but I had to know.

Saad took a handful of something out of his pocket and put it under the nose of one of his lambs. The lamb went for it and started to munch noisily. Then Saad walked over to the flat stone and the lamb followed him there bleating for more of the good stuff as it went. When they reached the stone, Saad struck with the speed and precision of a snake. In a flash, he took the lamb by the front feet and looped the rope around them. He pulled and the lamb fell to the ground and landed on its side. Next Saad tied the back feet to the front. He did it so fast I could not keep up with him. The lamb bleated and struggled, trying to get up, but it couldn't. Saad had it by one of its horns now. It was helpless.

Then from nowhere, a long black knife suddenly appeared in Saad's hand. I had no idea where it came from. Did he have it stuck in his black boot, or was it up his sleeve? Did he have it inside his shirt, or was it hidden in the pocket of his baggy pants? I could not tell, but there it was in his hand, and he was mumbling something over the lamb. I thought I heard him say, "In the name of Allah, who has made you *halal* (kosher) for us to slay and eat." And then down came the raised hand upon the wooly throat. One pass, two passes, three and four and red blood shot from the lambs throat like a geyser. It came in spurts that made my guts hurt. But the spurts got weaker and weaker until they finally became only a slow ooze. The lamb shuddered as it tried to breathe, but all I could hear was a gurgling in the throat.

It sickened me and my knees got weak. For a moment I thought I was going to pass out. I leaned against my mother and held tightly on to her hand. Then I looked over at the rest of the flock. They were still grazing on the shoulder of the road. They did not stop or even slow down while one of them bled to death on the cold flat stone less than ten yards away. What I saw that morning has always been with me, like a sore that never heals. And I wondered why it had to be that way. Why did we have to kill to eat? But I never said anything to my mother or anybody else about it. What was there to say? They had been doing it all their lives, and they never saw anything wrong with it.

When the lamb finally stopped moving, Saad untied its feet and stuck the piece of rope in his pocket. He took the dead lamb by the hind foot and with his knife made a small cut in the ankle. He put his mouth to the cut and began to blow. The lamb, like a balloon, started to swell up. Saad blew and blew and the lamb grew larger and larger, like a goatskin full of wine. I asked my mother what he was doing, and she said that he was separating the hide from the flesh so the lamb would be easier to skin.

That was it for me. I could not take any more and I wandered off to the far end of the square where the old men of the village gathered to talk and smoke in the morning and late in the afternoon. It was getting light and some of the village women started to show up. The square was suddenly swarming with people like flies on a carcass. My mother got exactly what she came after that morning, and we headed home with a basketful of steaming warm ribs. I never saw Saad or his sheep after that. I never wanted to.

The last house before the olive press is Im Ayyoub's, one of the poorest women in the whole village. Im Ayyoub has nothing—no land, no trees, no olives. She doesn't even have a clothesline to hang her wash on. She just lays her clean clothes and bed sheets and towels on bushes here and there around her house to dry. But Im Ayyoub is smart, and she knows how to get what she wants and what her family needs. In her kitchen, there are four big clay jars full of olive oil and pickled olives, more than she can possibly need before the next season. She gets her olives by trading with the village kids. One cup of her delicious salted lupini beans for one cup of fat ripe olives, black or green. That is the deal. And she never asks any questions. When my friends and I show up at her door with our pockets full of olives, she does not ask us where the olives came from, and we don't offer to tell her. We empty our pockets silently in her tin can and she shakes it a few times to make the olives settle. Then she gives us an equal measure of her tasty yellow beans.

From where I am now, I cannot see the olive press, but I can smell it. A few more steps, around Abu Sami's stone wall, and I see it, a square, flat-topped stone building by the old cypress tree. Now I am running.

When I go into the olive press, I feel as if I am entering a cave. It is cool and dark inside. It takes a moment for my eyes to adjust. Now I can see a little in the light of the dawn.

"Well, well, well. Aren't we up early this morning, and with an armful of bread, too."

I can barely make out the silhouette of the man, but I know who he is immediately. I recognize the voice. It is that of Abu Fareed, the storekeeper. During olive season Abu Fareed operates the capstan at the olive press. If somebody wants to buy something, like a pack of cigarettes or a bag of sugar, it's no problem. Abu Fareed drops whatever he is doing, walks over to his store, and gets it. Then, rubbing his nose with his long index finger, he saunters back to his post at the capstan. He is tall and thin. His shoulders are hunched. And he takes long leisurely strides. I have never seen him move fast. Abu Fareed is never in a hurry.

"Good morning, Abu Fareed," I say. "I am not too early, am I?"

"And a good morning to you, Anwar, son of Fuad, son of Hassan. No, you're definitely not too early. In fact, you're just in time. The first batch is coming in right now." I edge forward. I hear a familiar snort to my right. I see Abu Asaad's old white mare standing at the far end of the press first. Then I see Abu Asaad, the mule skinner, hanging a bag of feed around his mare's neck. I did not notice them at first because they are quiet. They are taking a break from going round and round and pulling the huge stone that crushes the olives into a pulp. The mare goes in front and Abu Asaad walks behind her every step of the way. When he stops, she stops. When he moves, she moves. That's the way it has been for years. That's the way it has always been with everybody in Magdaluna. Everything that the village did was as predictable as the seasons and the rising and the setting of the sun. Here life is sure-footed. It is certain. And I feel safe.

"Whose olives are these?" I ask Abu Fareed.

He rubs his nose with a straight finger. "They're the widow Farha's. She brought them in early this morning and went back to her house to feed her chickens. She should be back any minute now."

I watch Abu Fareed at work. He takes a square sheet made from woven goat hair. It is about one yard wide and one and a half yards long. He scoops some crushed olive pulp and places it on the sheet. Then he spreads the pulp around into an even layer and folds the edges of the sheet in. He takes this last square and places it on the pile of other squares just like it, which he had stacked before I showed up. He walks over to the corner and grabs a long straight wooden rod bigger around than my arm. He sticks the rod into a hole in the capstan, and turns. The capstan creaks and the round pad moves down slowly. Abu Fareed takes the rod out and sticks it into another hole. He turns it again and the top pad descends some more. One more turn and the top pad is down on the pile of sheets full of pulp. Another turn and the oil begins to flow. It gushes out of the spout on the front of the capstan. The sun is up now and the morning light spills in through the eastern window and falls on the cataract of oil. The capstan squeals as it turns, the wood groans, and the oil flows, thick and opaque and green. The aroma fills the room. It fills my lungs, and I shudder with joy. I feel that I am witnessing something very good, very old and . . . holy. My arms are covered with goose bumps. Then I become aware that I am glad to be alive . . . that I am here. Abu Fareed's voice calls me back.

"Come over here and give me a hand, son. This is getting tight now. I can use some help."

I am happy to be asked. And I put all my weight behind the wooden beam. Down goes the pad and out flows the oil like molten gold in the morning sun. Abu Asaad comes over, and the three of us squeeze until there is nothing to squeeze anymore.

We are breathing hard. We stop and stand with our hands resting on our hips and look at the vat under the spout. It is a pool of emerald green. The vat is full to the brim with the fat and the goodness of the earth, and the whole world smells of fresh olive oil.

As soon as we have rested a little, Abu Fareed says to me, "Now where is that bread of yours, son of Fuad? Bring it over here to me."

I pick it up off the bench by the door where I had set it down and hand it to him. He carefully unwraps it the way a priest does communion bread and he takes one sheet of *marquq* bread out. He casts it on the surface of the oil like a fisherman casts his net on the water. It floats. Now he takes it by the edge and turns it over. He lets it soak up the oil for a moment or two. Then he lifts it out of the vat, rolls it up neatly, and squeezes the excess oil out of it. This is the moment I have waited for all summer—my first bite of village bread soaked in fresh virgin olive oil. My mouth waters. My jaws ache a little. Abu Fareed hands me the dripping tortilla and says, "*Sahtain*, son. Eat it in good health." I receive it from his hand as the widow Farha walks in. I greet her. Then in keeping with custom, I say to her, "May God bless your harvest and multiply it so that you shall have no room." The widow Farha says Amen and casts her bread upon the oil to give to Abu Fareed and Abu Asaad. All four of us stand silently around the vat and eat the first fruit of the season. None of us utters a word, but we all know that nothing on God's earth tastes like hot fresh olive oil and village bread in the early sun of a September morn.

13

The Telephone

FOR AS FAR BACK as anybody in the Tower of the Moon could remember, time had never really meant much except maybe to those who were dying or those who were waiting to appear in court before a *qadhi* (judge) because they had tampered with the boundary markers on their land. In those days there was no real need for a calendar or a watch to keep track of the hours, days, months, and years. We knew what to do and when to do it just as the geese knew when to fly north, driven by the hot *Janoubiah* (southerly) wind that blew in from the desert, and the ewes knew when to give birth to their wet lambs that stood on long, shaky legs in the chilly wind of March and baaed hesitantly because they were small and cold and did not know where they were or what to do now that they were here.

The only timepiece that we ever had need of then was the sun. It rose and it set and the seasons rolled by and we sowed seed and harvested and ate and played and married our cousins and had babies who had whooping cough and chicken pox, and those who survived grew up and married their cousins and had children who had whooping cough and chicken pox. We lived

and loved and toiled and died to the beat of a distant and name-
less drummer without ever needing to know what year it was or
even the time of day.

It wasn't that we had no system for keeping track of time
and the important events in our lives. But ours was a natural,
or, rather, a divine calendar, it was framed by acts of God.
Allah Himself set down the milestones with earthquakes and
droughts and floods and locusts and pestilence. Simple as it
was, our calendar worked just fine for us.

Take, for example, the birth of Im Khalil, who was the oldest
woman in Magdaluna and all the surrounding villages. She was
so old that the skin of her cheeks looked like my father's grimy
tobacco pouch. When she came to visit, I had to kiss her because Grandma insisted that I show her old friend affection. It
was like kissing a soft suede leather glove that had been sweated
through and then left in a dark closet for a season. Teta Im Khalil's face roused my curiosity and got me to wondering one day
how old one had to be to look and taste the way she did. As soon
as she got up and hobbled off on her cane, I asked Grandma,
"How old is Teta Im Khalil?"

Grandma had to think for a moment. Her lips moved while
she thought, then she said, "I've been told that Teta was born
shortly after the big rainstorm that caused the roof on the may-
or's house to cave in."

"And when was that?" I asked.

"Oh, about the time we had the big earthquake that cracked
the wall in the east room."

Well, that did it for me. You couldn't be more accurate than that, now, could you? Satisfied with her answer, I went back to playing with a ball made from an old sock stuffed with other, much older socks.

And that's the way it was in our little village for as long as anybody could remember. People were born so many years before or after an earthquake or a flood. They got married or died so many years before or after a long drought or a big snow or some other disaster. But one of the most unusual of these dates was when Antoinette, the weaver's daughter, and Saeed, the barber, got married. That was the year of the whirlwind when fish and oranges fell from the sky. Incredible as it may sound, the story of the fish and oranges was true because men, respectable men, like Abu George, the farrier, and Abu Asaad, the mule skinner—men who would not lie, not even to save their own souls, told and retold that story until it was incorporated into Magdaluna's calendar like the year of the black moon and the year of the locusts before it. My father, too, confirmed the story to me. He told me that he had been a small boy himself when it rained fish and oranges from heaven. He had gotten up one morning after a stormy night and walked out into the yard to find fish as long as his forearm, still flopping here and there among wet navel oranges.

The year of the fish-bearing twister, however, was not the last of the remarkable years. Many others followed in which strange and wonderful things happened, and many more milestones were added by the hand of Allah to Magdaluna's cosmic calendar. There was, for instance, the year of the drought, when heaven was shut for months and the spring from which the entire village got its drinking water slowed to a trickle. The spring was about a mile from the village in a ravine that opened on the northeastern end into a small, flat clearing that was always covered with fine gray dust and hard marble-size goat droppings, because the goatherds brought their flocks there every afternoon to water them.

In the year of the drought, that little clearing was always packed full of noisy little kids with big brown eyes and sticky hands and their mothers, sinewy, overworked young women with protruding collarbones and deep-cracked, calloused brown heels. The children ran around and played tag or hide-and-seek while the women talked, shooed away flies, and waited for their turn to fill up their jars with drinking water to take back home to their napping men and wet babies. There were days when we had to wait from sunup until late in the afternoon just to fill a small clay jar with precious cool water.

Sometimes amid the long wait and the heat and the flies and the smell of goat dung, tempers flared, and the younger women, who were anxious about their babies, argued over whose turn it was to fill up her jar. Sometimes the arguments turned into full-blown knockdown and drag-out fights; the women would grab each other by the hair and curse and scream and spit and call each other names that made my ears tingle. We little brown boys who went with our mothers to fetch water loved these fights because we got to see the women's legs and their colored panties as they grappled and rolled around in the dust. Once in a while we got lucky and we got to see much more than that because some of the women wore nothing at all under their long dresses.

God, I remember how I used to look forward to these fights. I remember the rush, the excitement, the sun dancing on the dust clouds, a dress ripped, a young white breast revealed and quickly hidden. In my calendar, that year of drought will always be one of the best years of my childhood because it was then, in a dusty clearing by a trickling mountain spring, I got some of my first glimpses of the mysteries and promises hidden within the folds of a woman's dress. Fish and oranges from heaven . . . you can get over that.

But in another way, the year of the drought was also one of the worst years of my life because it was in that year that Abu Raja, the retired cook who used to entertain us kids by cracking walnuts on his forehead, decided that it was about time Magdaluna got its own telephone. He said every civilized village needed one, and Magdaluna was not going to get anywhere until it got a telephone, its link with the outside world. I was too young to understand what was going on at the time, but a few men like Shukri, the retired Turkish drill sergeant, and Abu Jameel, the vineyard keeper, did all they could to talk Abu Raja out of having a telephone brought to the village. But they were outshouted and ignored and finally shunned by the other villagers because they resisted progress and did not want a good thing to come to Magdaluna.

It was a warm day in the early fall and many of the village people were in their fields repairing walls or gathering wood for

the winter when the shout went out that the telephone company men had arrived at Abu Raja's country store, which used
to be a bedroom before Abu Raja retired and decided to go into
the storekeeping business.

Abu George, who had a huge voice and, until the telephone
showed up, was Magdaluna's only long-distance communications system, bellowed the news of the men's arrival from his
front porch. Everybody dropped whatever they were doing and
ran to Abu Raja's house by the threshing floor to see what was
happening. But some of the more dignified villagers, like Abu
Milhem and Abu Na'im, who had been to big cities like Beirut
and Damascus and had seen things like telephones and tele-
graphs, did not run the way the rest of us did. They just walked,
looking straight ahead, their canes hanging from the crooks of
their arms as if they were going for a Sunday afternoon stroll.

It did not take long for the whole village to assemble at Abu
Raja's *dikkan* in order not to miss that historic moment. Some
of the rich villagers, like the widow Farha, and the gendarme,
Abu Nadeem, did not hesitate to walk into the store and stand
at the elbows of the two very important-looking men who pro-
ceeded with utmost dignity, like priests at communion, to wire
the telephone. The poor villagers stood outside and listened
carefully to what was being relayed to them by the not-so-poor
people who stood in the doorway and were in a position to see
what was happening inside.

"The bald man is cutting the blue wire," someone said.

"He is sticking the wire into the hole in the bottom of the
black box," someone else added.

"The telephone man with the mustache is connecting two pieces of wire. He is twisting the ends together," a third voice chimed in.

Because I was small and unaware of the fact that I was poor and should have stood outside with the other poor folk to give the rich people inside more room, which they seemed to need more of than the poor people did, I wiggled my way through the dense forest of legs to get a firsthand look at what was going on. It was awesome. I felt like the barefoot Moses when he stood, sandals in hand, looking at the burning bush on Mount Sinai. Breathless, I watched the men in blue, with fancy lettering in a foreign language on their shirt pockets, put together a black machine that would make it possible to talk with uncles, aunts, and cousins who lived more than two days' ride away.

It was a little after sunset when the man with the mustache announced that the telephone was now ready to use. He told Abu Raja that all he had to do was lift the receiver and turn the crank on the black box a few times and wait for an operator to take his call. Abu Raja, who had lived and worked in the big city on the coast, got a little impatient with the telephone man who assumed that he was ignorant. He grabbed the receiver and turned the crank with force, as if he was trying to start a model A Ford. Everybody was impressed because he knew what he was doing. He even knew the operator personally and called her by her first name—*Centralist* (French for operator).

Within a few minutes Abu Raja was talking with Michel, his brother, who was a concierge in Beirut. Abu Raja didn't even have to raise his voice or shout to be heard. Can you imagine that? Beirut! If I hadn't seen it with my own two eyes and heard it with my own two ears, I would not have believed it. My friend Kameel didn't. He was away that day, watching his father's goats, and he did not believe it when he came back to the village that evening. His cousin Habeeb and I ran to meet him and tell him about the telephone and how Abu Raja had used it to speak with his brother in Beirut. When he heard us say that, he made the sign of the cross and kissed his thumbnail. Then he told us that lying was a bad sin and it would surely get us into purgatory.

Kameel believed in Jesus and Mary and he wanted to be a priest when he grew up. He always crossed himself when Habeeb, who was irreverent, and I, who was Presbyterian, were around, even when we were not bearing bad news. But the telephone, as it turned out, was bad news. After its coming, the face of the village began to change.

One of the first things that the coming of the telephone did to Magdaluna was to shift its center. Before it came, the men of the village used to get together at Im Kaleem's, their favorite haunt. Their hostess, Im Kaleem, was a short, middle-aged widow who had jet black hair and a raspy voice that could be heard all over the village even when she was only whispering. She was a devout Catholic and she also was the village *shlikki* (whore). Her house was at the entrance of the village, and the men met there to argue about politics and to drink coffee and play cards or *tawli*. Im Kaleem was not a prostitute, however, because she did not charge for her services, not even for the coffee and tea and occasionally the *arrack* that she served her men friends. She did not need the money. Her boy, who was overseas somewhere in Africa, sent her money regularly. I know because my father used to read his letters to her and he would write her boy back because she could not read or write. Im Kaleem was not a slut either, like some of the other women in the village, because she loved all the men that she entertained and they loved her back, every one of them. She was kind of married to all the men in the village. Everybody knew it. The wives knew it and the Catholic priest knew it and the Presbyterian minister knew it, but nobody seemed to mind. Actually, there were times when I suspected that the women, including my mother, who wrung their hands unconvincingly and complained to one another about their men's unfaithfulness, secretly did not mind their husbands' visits to Im Kaleem because that kept the men out of their hair while they attended to their endless chores. Im Kaleem was also great for talking sense to those men who were having family problems. She was a kind of sister confessor and troubleshooter, especially for the younger couples, who seemed to have more fights than the older folks.

Before the telephone came to Magdaluna, Im Kaleem's house saw a lot of hustle and bustle at just about any time of the day and especially at night when it was always brightly lit with three large kerosene lamps, and the loud voices of the men talking, laughing, and arguing, heard from the street below, sounded reassuring and homey. Her house, especially in the evenings, was a little island of comfort, an oasis for the weary village men who were exhausted from having so little to do.

It wasn't long before many of these men, the younger ones especially, started spending more of their days and evenings at Abu Raja's *dikkan*. They would eat and drink and talk and play checkers and *tawli* and lean their chairs back against the wall, which signaled that they were ready to throw back and forth at each other, like a ball, the latest rumors going around in the village, always looking up from their games and drinks and glancing at the phone in the corner as if they were expecting it to ring any minute and bring them news that would change their lives and deliver them from their aimless existence.

They waited for the calls to come and in the meantime smoked cheap hand-rolled cigarettes, dug the dirt from under their fingernails with big pocket knives, and drank lukewarm sodas, beer, and *arrack*. Sometimes the days dragged on so very slowly, especially when it got hot, and that was when the men turned on Najib, the confirmed bachelor who practically lived in Abu Raja's *dikkan*, and started to poke fun at him and tease him because he'd been going around barefoot and unshaven since the Virgin appeared to him behind the olive press the year his mother slipped in the church yard, broke her hip, and died.

The telephone was bad news for me too. It took away from me a lucrative business—a source of steady and much-needed income. Before it came to Magdaluna, I used to hang around Im Kaleem's courtyard and play marbles with the other kids, waiting for someone to call down from the window of the upper room, where the men gathered, and ask me to run to the store to get them cigarettes or *arrack*, or to deliver a message to their wives, like telling them what they wanted for supper. There was always something in it for me like a ten or even twenty-five plaster piece. On a good day, I ran nine or ten of those errands, which meant a steady supply of candy and marbles, which I usually lost to Hani or his cousin Sami.

The telephone changed all that. Fewer and fewer men seemed to come to Im Kaleem's as the days went by because now they congregated at Abu Raja's to wait by the telephone. In the evenings, there was no light falling from her window on the street below, and the laughter and the noise that the men used to make trailed off and finally stopped. Only Shukri, the Turkish army drill sergeant, remained faithful to Im Kaleem after all the other men deserted her, and he was seen going into her house or leaving it from time to time. Early that winter Im Kaleem suddenly turned gray. She got sick and old. Her legs started giving her trouble and she could barely walk. By spring she was hardly ever seen outside her house anymore.

Oh, yes, the calls did eventually come, as expected, and the men and women started leaving the village like the falling of hail. First one, then two, then in bunches. The army took them. Domestic service in the cities took them. And ships and airplanes carried them to far away places like Australia and Brazil and New Zealand. Kameel the goatherd's son, his cousin Habeeb, and their cousins and my cousins all went away to become ditch diggers and mechanics and butcher shop boys and deli owners who wore dirty aprons sixteen hours a day, always looking for a better life than the one they had left behind. Within a year, many of the young men and women were gone. The sick, the old, and the maimed were left behind.

Magdaluna became a skeleton of its former self, desolate and forsaken, like the tombs, a place to get away from.

The telephone was the siren's call, but it was the car, the magic carpet of the twentieth century, that would come to the village and eventually carry it away.

14

The Car

THERE WERE only four us of at the village spring that day:
Sami, the basket weaver's boy who had lost one eye when his
mother, Salma, the seamstress, let him play with her scissors
when he was just a tot; Kameel the goatherd's son, who wanted
to be a priest when he grew up; his first cousin Habeeb, who did
not bother to make any future plans because he knew he was
never going to make it to nineteen, as his mother told him over
and over again, and I, the son of the Turkish one, as Abu George
called me. Kameel was watching his father's goats that day
because his father had been having chest pains. Habeeb, Sami,
and I were just hanging around the spring because it was *Ab*
(August) and it was hot.

All four of us were sitting at the edge of the stone trough with
our bare feet stuck in the cool, clear water up to our knees. It was
a lazy summer afternoon, the kind that sucks up all your ener-
gies and leaves you wanting to do nothing but lounge around,
chew on a straw or sour grass, and listen to the even drone of the
wasps and the bees in the clover. None of us had any idea that
in a few minutes, Abu Ameer, the village tinkerer and snitch,

would be coming down to the spring to fill his jar and change our lives forever.

He sneaked up on us, as was his habit, and said, "Hey, you boys! You haven't been playing with yourselves, now, have you? You know that hair will grow on your palms if you do, don't you?"

Well, we didn't know. So the four of us flipped our brown wet hands over and looked for the hair on our palms. There was none there. Then we looked up at him and saw him grinning from ear to ear. The son of a bitch had us again. And he laughed. We hung our heads down like stupid sheep and waited for him to get done and go away. While his jar was filling up, he sat on a flat rock by the spring and waited. He was quiet for a while. Then he spoke, "I guess you haven't heard about the *machana* that's up on the threshing floor, have you boys?" Habeeb said, "What *machana*? We've heard nothing about any *machana*. And what in the world is a *machana* anyway?"

Abu Ameer, his hands busy rolling a cigarette, said, "It's an *automobile*—a DeSoto. Don't you heathens know anything? What have you been learning in school anyway? Hasn't Master Butros been teaching you anything? Eh?"

"Nothing about any *machanas*, that's for sure," I said. "But I've heard my father talk about horseless carriages that run on something like lamp oil. He said they can go faster than the wind. But I didn't pay him any attention because he's always saying stuff like that which doesn't make any sense. He told me about tanks he'd seen in the Big War that can go anywhere they wanted to and drive right through stone buildings. Can you believe that? How can anything go through a building?"

"Well, I don't know what your father's been telling you, boy," said the snitch, "but if you want to see a *machana* you've got to go up to the threshing floor by Abu Fareed's *dikkan*. There is a *machana* parked there now. Haleem, the preacher's son, drove it up from Sidon. He's driving it back down there first thing tomorrow morning. So, you'd better hurry and get up there if you want to see it."

I did not trust that man, Abu Ameer. Never did. He was always pulling our legs and telling us fibs. He was the one who tricked me and stole my sandwiches from me when I was little. But the desire to see this new thing called *machana* was more than I could resist. I looked at Habeeb and he looked back at me. We were thinking the same thing. He got up and said, "I'll race you guys to the top of the hill," and took off without giving Sami or me a chance to pull our sandals back on our wet feet. Habeeb was barefoot as he usually was in summer, and he ran like a gazelle. I ran after him, hollering for him to wait up. He wouldn't. Kameel could not come with us. He had to stay behind because he could not leave his father's goats unattended. Someone might steal one of his kids and eat it, or the jackals might carry one away. I looked back just as we topped the hill and I saw him standing with his shepherd's staff in his hand looking up longingly after us.

The threshing floor was just beyond the top of the hill. There was a large natural pond between it and the hill. Except for a muddy brown hole in its center, the pond was dry from early June until late September, when the first autumn rain fell and filled it back up again. Habeeb ran across the dry, cracked bed around the hole. Sami and I were right behind him, fast on his heels. Abu Fareed's *dikkan* was just beyond the bank. Sweating and panting, we scrambled up the bank, grabbing onto shrubs and dry clumps of grass. When we topped the bank we could not see the *machana*. We had to walk around the store to the front, and even then we could not see it. It was hidden from view by a large crowd standing around it. I think everybody in the village was there that day, and nobody was saying a word. When someone spoke it was in whispers, as if they did not want to wake up the *thing* in their midst.

I wanted to see what it was. I stood on my tiptoes, but I couldn't see it. There were too many grown-ups between me and the thing. I jumped up to catch a glance of it, but I couldn't jump high enough. So, I did the only thing left for me to do. I pushed through the dense forest of warm, sweaty bodies and got in. Then I saw it—a big black thing, as big as a mountain of charcoal. It was gleaming like a ripe, black olive in the sun. I stopped breathing. Then everything around me slowly began to fade away until nothing was left but that *machana* and I. I had no idea how long I had been standing there, oblivious of everything and everyone around me, when a man's voice broke through my trance, as if it was coming from a far away place. The voice said, "You want a ride? Hey, you, Anwar, son of Fuad, I'm talking to you. You want to go for a spin?" I could not speak. I just nodded my head to mean yes. Haleem said, "Okay, boys, I can't take all of you at once. We'll have to do this in shifts, all right? Everybody gets to ride, but we'll have to do it in turn. Now you boys (pointing in my direction) you are the youngest, aren't you? You get to go first." Habeeb, Sami, and I stepped forward. Two or three other kids did too, but I wasn't looking. Then Haleem said, "You're not going to ride *inside* my automobile, you hear? It's clean and I don't want it messed up. You'll have to ride on the running boards. See? This is how you do it. You step up here and hold on to the doorpost like this. You understand? Hold on tight. I don't want anybody getting hurt."

I was up on that running board before he was finished talking, and I hooked my arm around the doorpost and hugged it tight. As soon as the other kids were on board, Haleem got into his *machana* and started it. There was a rumble as loud as God's thunder, but I did not let go and run like Sami and Habeeb did. I just closed my eyes and hung on to that doorpost for dear life. Then the thunder got even louder and the *machana* began to move forward, slowly at first. Haleem shouted, "Hold on, boys. Here we go," and the *machana* took off like a bull that's been bitten on the ass by a horsefly. I mean it moved. I had never seen the world go by so fast in my whole life. My lungs were filled to bursting with air. My shirt puffed up on my back, and my skin felt fresh and cool.

I started laughing. I laughed and the other kids laughed, and I wanted the ride on the running board of Haleem's *machana* to go on forever. I didn't want it to stop, ever. But it did all too soon. After we'd gone three laps around the threshing floor, Haleem stopped. He said, "Well, how did you like it, boys?

Wasn't it fun? Did you have a good time?" But none of us could speak. We just nodded our heads. All I could do was raise my hand and place it on my heart in a gesture of thanks. We stepped back to let the next group of boys and girls have their ride.

I relived my thrill over and over again that afternoon watching the other kids have their turn riding the *machana*. Finally, Haleem pulled up to Abu Fareed's *dikkan* and stopped. He got out and said, "That's it for today. I've got to go home now. I don't want any of you boys messing with my automobile, you hear? You can look but you cannot touch, all right? No touching." Then he left. The crowd slowly dispersed. The heat was unbearable and they left for the comfort of their cool homes.

But I didn't. I couldn't. I stood in front of Haleem's automobile and stared into its glass eyes. I drew closer to where the rumbling noise had come from and sniffed it. I had never before smelled anything like that *machana* before. Someone said it was gasoline I was smelling and I loved it. It was a mysterious smell, this smell of speed, this fragrance of power. I filled my lungs with it again and again until I got lightheaded. I was high on Haleem's *machana*.

I kept that high for the rest of the day and the evening. I went to bed that night, but I could not sleep thinking about the awesome black machine parked on the threshing floor by Abu Fareed's store. There was a picture of the Good Shepherd on the western wall facing my bed, and when I looked at it the thought came to me that if Jesus had stormed into Jerusalem in a *machana* like Haleem's instead of riding on the back of an ass, He might have won. I studied the portrait and pictured the Lord rumbling into Jerusalem in a massive black DeSoto with his disciples Peter, John, Thomas, Judas, and the rest of the bunch riding the running boards on either side of him and scaring the daylights out of the Romans, the tax collectors, and the priests. That would have been something to behold. *That* would have been a real miracle that no one, Roman, Greek, or Jew, could have stood up to or argued with.

Who knows what would have happened if Jesus had had one of those mean machines? He might even be still alive today. I also thought about the men who had made this smoke-belching *machana* that moved faster than the wind. I wondered if they were giants, bigger and taller than Samson or Goliath, whose stories Grandma had told me time and time again. I wondered what those giants wore, what they ate, and what kind of houses they lived in. When I finally drifted off to sleep, I dreamt that I was flying all over the land.

When I woke early the next morning, the world was a much bigger and more wonderful place than it was before Haleem's *machana* came to my little village. Things—strange and wonder-full things—were happening in another world beyond the blue mountains of Joun in the east and the foggy Abulyabis River in the west. And I wanted to know that world out there. I ached to see it.

I did. Within two years the world beyond the river and the hills came rushing into mine like a great and mighty wind. It was such a swift and violent wind that it leveled everything in its path—nothing was left standing—nothing.

A couple of months after Haleem's automobile came to Magdaluna, Majeed, the mayor's son bought one, a newer model. Then Saeed the barber got himself an old blue Ford whose color was faded in spots over the hood in the front and the trunk in the back. And Bahjat and his brother Sim'an pooled the money they'd saved for years working at their father's gristmill and got themselves an old DeSoto too. Their wives, who used to be close before their husbands bought the car, never got along after that because they could not agree on who would have it on certain days. But the men were happy they had *their* car to wash, to tinker with, and to ride around in. God, how they loved to toot their horn.

Finally, Fareed, the son of the store keeper, got himself an old bus, a big, ugly, green bus, that had a hole in its floor. He thought that there was money to be made ferrying people back and forth between Magdaluna and Sidon, the big city ten miles away down on the coast. He was right. He made a killing taking a busload of people to Sidon in the morning and bringing them back in the evening around sundown.

Now the village people, who for as far back as anyone could remember had managed to live comfortably in their little self-contained microcosm, could not live without *stuff* that they could get only in Sidon. Take pita (pocket) bread, for instance. When Sidon became only a hop, skip, and jump away, pita became the bread of choice. The village women, including my mother, did not want to be bothered anymore. They did not see the point in making dough and kneading it and baking village bread. Why bother, they said, when city bread was just a few hours away? All the women had to do was give Fareed a list of the things they needed and he would pick them up and bring them back with him in the evening. The women were happy to have their city stuff, and he made a little money delivering it to them.

Things got even easier as time went by, and a lot of the back-breaking work, which the villagers had to do before the automobile changed everything, became unnecessary. No one needed to can fruit or vegetables or make preserves anymore. Why make homemade fig or quince or apricot preserves when you could get all that right out of a tin can? Why plant wheat and harvest it and take it to the mill to have it ground into flour when good city bread could be bought fresh every day? None of the women wanted to make their dresses anymore. They could go down on Fareed's bus in the morning and buy the latest fashions from a clothing store in Sidon right off the rack.

Before you knew it, Abu Antoun, the cobbler, and Salma, the seamstress, went out of business. Saad, the traveling butcher stopped coming to Magdaluna on Saturday mornings to slaughter his lambs and sell their meat in the village square. After the car and the bus came to Magdaluna, meat could be bought any day of the week. Instead of eating it once or twice a week, as they used to, the villagers could eat meat seven days a week if they wanted to. Fish, too, was no longer a rare treat that we ate every other week in the summer. We could get lots of it in Sidon any time we had a yen for it. Nothing was too far away or unavailable anymore. In a pinch, a man could drive down to Sidon for a box of matches and a pack of cigarettes. Planning ahead to avoid being caught short or running out of things was

no longer called for. Magdalunians went from long-term planning to day-by-day living in no time at all.

But all that convenience and abundance came at a price.
The village had to redesign itself around its increasing cars and
buses. Wider roads were needed. Olive trees and carob trees
and other fruit-bearing trees like plum and apple and pome-
granate trees that were as old as the village itself had to be felled.
Stone houses and walls that had been in the village for generations had to be torn down. When new houses were built, they
were built with the car in mind. A man could not put his house
anywhere he pleased on his property anymore. He had to
accommodate the car, whether it was his or someone else's.
One thing was sure—the car had the right of way. There were
taxes—road building and road maintenance taxes—to be paid
to keep the car on the road. And death. The car, like a malevo-
lent pagan god, demanded human sacrifice. It exacted offerings
of flesh and blood, especially young flesh and blood. The first
victim of the car was Jameel, the son of Abu Jameel, Magdaluna's vineyard keeper.

For six years, I was told, Abu Jameel and his wife had tried for
a boy because a son in our village was more precious than gold.
Magdalunians used to say that he who begets sons shall never
die, and he who does not have a son is dead already and his
memory shall be wiped out from the face of the earth. But every
summer Im Jameel delivered a healthy, bouncing baby girl, and
there was a lot of lamentation, chest beating, and gnashing of
teeth at Abu Jameel's house that day. Sometimes Abu Jameel's

neighbors joined him and his wife in the mourning that followed the birth of another baby girl.

Each year, Abu Jameel's reaction was worse than the year before, and when his sixth girl was born, he got so mad that he loaded his twelve-gauge, double-barreled shotgun, pointed it at heaven, and shot at Allah twice. He also spouted things that were incomprehensible because he had a lisp and he was hopping mad. Eleven months later, Im Fadel, the midwife, pulled a big baby boy out of Im Jameel and the whole village rejoiced. There was singing, dancing, yodeling, and feasting for days afterwards. Abu Jameel was ecstatic and felt vindicated. He had finally managed to get God's attention and got himself an heir to carry on his name so that his seed would not be cut off from the land forever. The baby was called Jameel after his grandfather and that was how his father and mother came to be called Abu Jameel and Im Jameel (*Abu* means *the father of*, and *Im* means *the mother of*).

Jameel grew up to be everything that a father would want his son to be. He was decent, obedient, honorable, and handsome. Because Jameel was his father's only son, he got just about anything he wanted, not that he was a demanding or unreasonable son. When he turned sixteen, he asked his father for a car because he needed it to go to school in Sidon. Abu Jameel did not hesitate for a moment. He sold a field on the outskirts of the village to the east and bought his son a little French car called Simca.

One cold and rainy evening when Jameel was on his way

home from school, he missed a turn on a dangerous curve, the Hyena's Shoulder, about three miles out of town. The Simca finally came to a stop at the bottom of a deep ravine after it had bounced and rolled for five or six hundred feet. There wasn't much left of the car or its driver by the time it slammed into the rocks at the bottom. Jameel was given the funeral of a prince. People came from all the villages around to honor him and his family. It was something that everyone would remember.

Jameel was the first victim, but there were many more after him. Not all of them died violent deaths like his; some were much slower and took a hell of a lot longer. Abu Nadi, for one, sucked up some fumes one cold winter day because the muffler of his old Dodge had a hole in it, and he started dying in 1951. It took him eleven years to succumb. I was told that he finally passed away in 1962, but by that time he was nothing but skin and bones and bedsores. Bahij, the son of the stonemason, was lucky. The car ate up only one of his fingers when his wedding ring was snagged by a fan belt, and Nadeem's neck was broken when he was looking for the source of a strange noise coming from under the hood of his car. His necktie was caught in a spinning pulley. He was luckier than some of the others, though. He healed nicely without suffering any permanent damage.

The last and probably the biggest victim of the *machana* was the village itself. Before the coming of the car, Magdaluna was a healthy and beautiful animal like a young tiger. Life made harsh demands on it, but the village rose to meet the challenge. It knew what to do and how to do it to survive. It had to know. There was no help from the outside. Magdaluna was a complete ecosystem, one of the last of a dying species, which was quietly being squeezed out of existence by modern technology and the cult of convenience. The village began to die when everyone in it became dependent on others and the things they made in far away places. There was no need anymore for anyone to learn to tan a hide, make carob molasses, or distill *arrack* from the vine. When old timers like Abu George, the blacksmith, and Abu Asaad, the mule skinner, passed away, there was nobody to take their place. Those who normally would have carried on were either not interested or already gone.

My family was not among the first to leave the village, but we, too, eventually answered the irresistible call. My father got word from an old army buddy that an oil company in South Lebanon was hiring interpreters. My father applied for a job and got it, and we moved to Sidon, where I went to a Presbyterian missionary school. Three years after graduation, having won a scholarship, I left Lebanon for the United States.

We had been among the last to leave the village to a slow and agonizing death. Whatever was left of the Tower of the Moon was destroyed during the Lebanese Civil War, which started in 1975 and lasted fifteen years. Moslem fighters came down from the eastern hills and ran off the last inhabitants left in Magdaluna. They blew its houses and churches up and leveled them to the ground with bulldozers. And to make sure that there would be no reason whatsoever for anybody to want to return to that desolation, they dug up the graves and scattered the bones of the dead here and there among the stumps of charred olive trees and fig trees.

In the early nineties, when a semblance of peace and order was restored, Uncle Wadi went back to Magdaluna and gathered the bones of his mother, Grandma Mariam, and the bones of my father, and those of Aunt Julia and Grandpa Hassan, who died before I was born. He put the bones back in the family grotto and resealed it with mortar and stone.

Whenever my mind drifts back to the days that are long gone, I find myself thinking about my old home, my father's bones, and my childhood. And in the very center of my many memories I see a shiny black DeSoto standing like a dark, massive monument upon what looks to me like the tomb of the world, the grave of us all.

~~❧~~

Returning

B Y T H E T I M E I returned to Lebanon with Gwen, my wife, in
September of 1969, Fate and Happenstance were already there
to meet us. They had been busy quarrying the boulders that I
was to add to my pyramid. They had been hard at it.

For the first three years back in Lebanon, my job was to teach
English at Gerard Institute, my alma mater. Our son was born
in 1971, at the end of those three years, and our daughter three
years after that, while I was teaching at the American University
of Beirut. Just after her birth, the Lebanese Civil War broke out
in February of 1975, a year that is filed in my memory as *The Year
of Our Lord Fear, Loss, and War.*

The war started with a fatal shot fired in Sidon, killing Ma'ar-
ouf Saad, a prominent Sidonian and deputy in the Lebanese
Parliament. Soon after that man's assassination, the war spread
to the rest of the country faster than a fire in a dry hayfield.
Within weeks, the whole country had gone berserk.

The Lebanese, who used to be the most fun-loving, easygo-
ing people in the Middle East, began to kill one another over a
loaf of bread, a gallon of gas, or religious persuasion. Armed

bands roamed the streets like packs of wild dogs. They did whatever they felt like doing. They took what they wanted and raped whom they pleased. The nightmare that would last fifteen years had just begun.

We were stuck in Sidon, about thirty-five miles south of Beirut.

We had chosen to remain there after I got my job at the AUB because my mother and my two sisters and their families lived there, and we felt safer in Sidon, where we were surrounded by relatives and friends. Also, it was cheaper to live in a small town than in Beirut. I used to commute to work at the university in a white Volkswagen Beetle, the first car we ever owned. But as the fighting escalated, my commutes to Beirut became less and less frequent and by the beginning of April I had completely given up on going to work. Being out on the road was a risk I could not afford to take.

Because our house in Sidon was strategically located on a hill overlooking the town, a band of armed thugs, some of them barely in their teens, chose to set up their machine guns, rocket launchers, and bazookas on our roof. With death encamped on top of us, and fear and confusion all around us, sleep became scarce, fresh bread a rare treat, and water, to drink or shower, more precious than Tennessee pearls.

We had missed our chance to get out. The American consulate had sent us word as early as March that it was no longer safe for us to remain in Sidon. But we could not afford to get out. We needed money to flee, and the banks were closed most of the time. We could not get to whatever little money we had to buy our way out. Most of the time it wasn't safe even to go out to the neighborhood grocery store, and sometimes the roads to Beirut would suddenly be barricaded by armed men who burned mountains of tires to stop traffic and to create an atmosphere of terror and confusion. At those barricades, many a good man and woman were shot on the spot or disappeared, never to be seen again, simply because their identification cards said that they were Christians. Some of those killed were acquaintances of mine; two were friends from school.

Our escape route was cut off. We could do nothing but hang around and wait for a break in the fighting. We whiled away the long days drinking Turkish coffee, listening to *My Word* on the BBC, watching reruns of Bonanza, and speculating about what might happen next.

In the meantime, we learned to recognize the different types of weapons by the sounds they made. We were good at it by April. Gwen could easily tell whether the shots we had just heard were made by a 16-millimeter gun, an M16, or a Kalashnikov, a Russian assault rifle also known as the AK 47.

Once in a while during this outbreak of insanity, Israeli fighter bombers would materialize from thin air and surgically remove a PLO base or ammo dump. One of those F11s flew by so close that Gwen could see the pilot's face behind the oxygen mask. Oh, God, how the earth trembled beneath our feet every time a silver rocket like a sliver of lightning slammed into the earth! Its very crust came alive and shuddered like a mule's hide when a green fly lights on it and stings. Following every explosion, sickening puffs of fetid wind washed over us like warm waves in a decaying sea.

Fuad, four, and Juli, barely one, learned fear very quickly and became adept at scampering around on all fours, like crabs, looking for a place to hide when they heard explosions that sounded close, and they were too damn close too much of the time. They also learned not to stand in the doorways or in front of windows where they could be spotted and picked off by some armed revolutionary kid taking target practice to test a new weapon or to improve his aim. Loud noises freaked our children out: a door banged or a window slammed shut by the wind would send them, like mice, scurrying for cover under a table or a bed, raw terror in their faces and unanswerable questions in their eyes. Our hearts were rent by the fear that took permanent residence in their pleading eyes and heaving chests. There was nothing we could do, nothing, except wait for a lull in the fighting so we could get out.

There was no way for us to get to the airport in Beirut until late in October. A brief respite in the fighting gave us our long-awaited break. I rented a taxi to take us to Beirut. To take us the thirty-mile trip to the airport, the cab driver asked for two hundred lira (about ninety dollars). He said he wouldn't do it for a piaster less because he was putting his life on the line. It was a bargain.

We managed to get to the airport with whatever little money and worldly possessions we had: two suitcases and a flight bag filled mainly with baby things such as diapers and bottles.

Everything else, including our books, our collection of Roman and Greek coins, and our record albums, had to be left behind. Our little *love bug*, with a Dumbo sticker on one door and Chip and Dale on the other, had been stolen, along with the rough draft and all my handwritten notes for my master's thesis, just two days before we left Sidon.

When we got to the airport, we were told that our plane, a Belgian Sabena Airlines flight, had overflown the country and landed in Amman, Jordan, because the airport in Beirut was under threat of bombardment.

There we were, stranded in the eye of the hurricane, waiting to be carried to safety by an airplane that would never come. The kids started crying because they were hot and scared and hungry, and my wife broke down and began to sob softly because she did not want to alarm the kids. She'd had about all she could take. Despair settled upon us like a wet, warm blanket. Breathing took a lot of effort. We desperately needed a miracle.

We got one in the form of the Reverend Elias Malki, minister of the Gospel and preacher of the Word of God. As we were sitting there in the pit of despair, Reverend Malki walked through the front gate of the airport, his face beaming with an enormous smile. We had met him the year before, and we had been to his English-speaking church in Beirut many times. This was a man in whose lexicon the word *fear* simply did not exist. His joy and bravery were contagious; we were thrilled to see him. He spotted us immediately and came to speak with us.

When he found out that we had no way out of Lebanon, he

took us in his station wagon to his apartment in downtown Beirut. He was living there with his youngest son, Danny, and his pet parrot. The rest of the Malkis had already fled to California.

That evening, Reverend Malki cooked supper for us and we went to bed early. We did not want to burn any lights at night because lights attracted bullets, just as a burning lamp attracts moths. Our sleep was fitful and interrupted because we kept hearing strange and horrible noises all night long—noises that ripped and sliced and tortured the silence of the cool, autumn night air.

Early the next morning Reverend Malki went to the neighborhood bakery and bought some steaming-fresh pita bread for breakfast. He fried eggs and made toast for us, hovering around us all the time, making sure that we had plenty to eat. It was the first time in weeks that we'd had fresh bread. I have not taken bread for granted since.

Later that day he drove to Amman, Jordan, where he bought us tickets on an Air Liban flight. That was the 28th of October, 1975, a day we will never forget because it was the day of our exodus—the day of our liberation from fear and the whims of evil men. We got out on the last Air Liban flight from Beirut that day.

After we were airborne, my wife breathed a huge sigh of relief. She was starting to feel a little at ease. She looked at me and said, "Thank God, we are out of danger now." She felt sad for me, though, when she saw the way I was looking out the window at the land we were leaving behind. She put her hand on my shoulder and said, "Are you taking one last look at your homeland?"

I said, "No, I am looking for SAM 6 ground-to-air missiles. They still can get us, you know."

The Mediterranean beneath us looked so benevolent, warm and . . . and sane. Lebanon was below us and behind forever. We took one last look at the blue mountains of what used to be my country and wept silently, as many of our fellow passengers were doing. My sisters Mary and Mona and their families were still down there. Nazira, my mother, and many others whom we loved were in that meat grinder below us. It was so hard to forsake them and leave what used to be the Middle East's Garden of Eden behind.

Having witnessed the death of a way of life, the extinction of a culture, was almost more than we could bear. But we were out at last, and we were safe.

It is the autumn of 1997 now. My life is more than half over, but my pyramid, which I have been building since 1947, when I first became aware of the world around me, is far from complete. It is enormous, though, as it stands now. The fiftieth tier, where I am today, is already tall enough to reach the silent darkness of cold space.

Fate and Happenstance have seen to it that my pyramid will be large enough to be fit for a king, yea even a god. Diligent they are, for they never slow down or tire. In fact, since I turned fifty, they have stepped up the pace. They seem to be bringing their gifts to me faster and faster every day. They must suppose that I can take what they dish out better than I used to when I was young. They keep pouring it on with no letup in sight. Sometimes willingly and sometimes reluctantly, but always relentlessly, they keep handing me big boulders too numerous to count, each representing an event—a happening.

There are so many that it boggles the mind just to think on them: incidents, accidents, people, coincidences, surprises, wars, books, romances, seasons, births, sunrises, hopes, deaths, feasts, hunger, seas, children, sunsets, disappointments, and dreams, some dead and buried but many unsurrendered—everything. I have crafted every boulder that was delivered unto me, all, in joy and in anguish, into polished stones, beautiful forever, and fitted them with love and with tears into the monument that stands for my mind's long journey, its trek up to the stars.

And I shall keep transforming what Fate and her half brother bring to me into precious stones and laying them in their places, perfect and everlasting—heat and pressure, heat and pressure, day in and day out, forever, until the I of me is gold and the heart of me is diamond. Then I will stand upon my pyramid pure and clean, for the fires of this hell, the sufferings of this world, will have cleansed me. And I will take my place among the stars of heaven for like them, I, too, shall be invincible.

A Word of Thanks

What or who could bring together seven individuals from so many different places to create a finished work of love? Could it be Fate? Was it Happenstance? Or perhaps it was entirely someone else whose unpronounceable name we do not even know? I can't even begin to guess. But the fact is that it happened, and *The Boy from the Tower of the Moon* was born. For that I shall forever be grateful.

My gratitude goes first and foremost to my wife, Gwendolyn Manheart Accawi, who urged me to write my stories about my village life "for the sake of the children." She welcomed each story with joy and sifted through it with eagle eyes looking for all the cracks and the holes before the kids even got to see it for the first time.

I am also indebted to my good friend Dr. Anthony K. Moses who, upon reading each rough draft would laugh, tap his pipe on the heel of his shoe, and say, "This is great! I love it! Send it off. Send it off, but first, you've got to tighten it up some more. Tighten it up." Mary Nietling, however, did not worry so much about tightening up the stories, but she pointed out the strengths and the weaknesses in each of them. She suggested doing away with the distractions—the things that got in the way of the story line. I will always be thankful for her enthusiasm and her untiring efforts. When I offered "The Telephone," one of my first stories, to *The Sun*, editors Sy Safransky and Andrew Snee said, "It is a wonderful story. We want it." They published it in their August 1997 issue, and the response since then has been beyond anything I had expected or imagined. Therefore, to Sy and Andrew, who took a chance on me and put the story out where it could be seen, goes my deep appreciation.

Finally comes the woman at the helm, Helene Atwan. I remember how happy I was when Helene first e-mailed me asking to see my manuscript.

Then I was thrilled when she called me to say "Let's get busy. We have a book to publish." With the spoked wheel firmly in hand, Helene steered *The Boy from the Tower of the Moon*, as one would a ship of the line, to its final safe haven, the hearts and minds of many. There are no words that can express my appreciation to her for having midwifed this my firstborn.

To these magnificent seven, including the mysterious choreographer who brought them together as a team, I say in gratitude and humility, "Thanks."